Act & Grow
RICH!

COMING SOON FROM
16 THINGS PRESS:

"Act & Grow Rich!" The Individual "Entrepreneurs"
& Business Owners Guide To Financial Freedom

"Act & Grow Rich!" App Series

"16 Things Kids Can Do To Act Right
& Help Save The Planet!"

Visit:
16ThingsKidsCanDo.Org
Working for The Betterment of
Kids, People & The Planet

Lyle Benjamin

ACT & GROW RICH!

The 99 Percenter's Guide On How To Grow & Protect Your Money, Tax-Free, Just Like The Wealthy

16 Things Press NY 2015

ACT & GROW RICH!
The 99 Percenter's Guide On How To Grow & Protect Your Money,
Tax-Free Just Like The Wealthy

16 THINGS PRESS
20 East Broadway, 4th Fl
New York, NY 10002
1-212-213-0257

Individual Sales. This book is available through most bookstores or can be ordered directly from ActandGrowRich.info.

Quantity Sales. Special discounts are available on quantity purchases by corporations, associations and others. For details, contact the "Special Sales Department" at the publisher's above address.

Printed in the United States of America
Library of Congress Cataloging-in-Publication Data
is available from the publisher
ISBN 0-9633386-5-5

Cover Design by Peijuan Tang & Lyle Benjamin
Interior Design by Lyle Benjamin

To Peijuan, Eric, Ryan
&
Friends & Families
Many of Whom I Have Yet To Meet

I Would Like To Offer A Special Thanks To
The Following People For Their
Assistance In Making This Book Happen:

Ilga Racika Racko, Hang Dong, Yafei Wang,
Rachel Dula & Charlotte Geslain

ON-LINE CONTENT
www.ActandGrowRich.info

ACTION ALERTS:

WORKBOOKS:

SURVEY:

The survey is available only on-line. Its purpose is to let us know what you think about various aspects of the book especially the concepts and programs, so we can work to improve our message.

Your feedback matters. It lets us know what we're doing wrong, right, and what we need to improve. So, it's much appreciated. Thank you.

CONTENTS

SECTION I:

THE DECK IS STACKED, THE GAME IS RIGGED, SO IT'S NOT OUR FAULT IF WE SUCK AT IT.

SECTION II:

HOW TO HARNESS YOUR PERSONAL POWER & UNLOCK YOUR HIDDEN MOJO!

SECTION III:

THE SECRET TO YOUR SUCCESS:
PART I. ALBERT EINSTEIN.

SECTION IV:

THE SECRET TO YOUR SUCCESS:
PART II. ROBERT KIYOSAKI.

Contents

SECTION V:

SUPPLEMENTAL MATERIALS.

#1. How To Have A Guaranteed Income For Life
#2. A Quick Guide To Planning Your Legacy
#3. Executive Bonus Plan
#4. Business Succession Planning
#5. Business Owner Buy/Sell Agreements

How To Win In America:

"Get Excited.
Become A Dreamer.
Feel Good About Yourself.
Don't Say I Can't.
Stand For Something.
Be Controversial.
Total Commitment To What You're About
   Regardless Of Success.
Learn To Treat People Well
Establish The Right Priorities.
God, Family And The Business.
Heart Of Champion, Never Quit.
Does Everything A Little More Than The Next Guy.
Must Be A Leader."
                     — Rich Thawley

"When when it comes down to it, we are all entreprenuers in our own right. We all need to learn and grow, we need to strive to do better in the future than we have done in the past. And to succeed, we must have a focus on the mission that motivates our goals and dreams."
— Lyle Benjamin

PREFACE

If you're looking for statistics and practical financial solutions you can use to help solve the problems you face as you struggle to achieve your financial goals ... this is the book for you.

On the other hand, if you're not so much into the numbers and the concrete concepts, and are more motivated by the emotional part of your brain ... we've got you covered too. Actually, most of this preface is for you.

Plus the other 40 chapters. Because, like it or not, you need to know the numbers "stuff" too. And more importantly, you need to act on it.

So whether you're "right" brain or "left" brain, I want you to ask yourself this question: "What is the pain it's going to cause me if I don't reach my financial goals?"

Put your life up on the screen like it's a movie, and really see what your life will be like if you don't achieve your financial objectives.

Instead of being able to eat out in any restaurant you choose, imagine being confined to eating microwave dinners at home, because you're counting your nickels and that's all you can budget.

Not able to afford a second home on the beach? Imagine having to sell your home, and move into the basement of your child's house, because you can't afford your own mortgage, taxes and insurance.

Instead of traveling around the world, will you be limited to just going to the Bingo Hall down the block?

Think about it. It's not a pretty picture. But this reality for millions of hard-working Americans who never imagined that their lives would turn out like they did.

Now think about this: There is a financial crisis in this country that has been building for decades upon decades. We have felt its tremors and suffered from its seemingly cataclysmic earthquakes. And each time we have crawled up out of the pit, inch by inch, month by month, year after year.

And we have listened to the pundits and the power brokers, the politicians and the educators, the liars and the snake oil salesman, and convinced ourselves that they hold the key to our salvation.

But year after year as we run along the path to our ultimate destination, the road is stretching out further and further into the distance. We are running harder and harder, while our rewards are fading into the haze of a distant future.

For the first time an entire generation of working-age children fears that they will not be able exceed the lifestyle of their parents.

The gap in this country is no longer between the rich and the poor: The gap is now between the rich and the middle class, and it's growing wider and wider with each passing year.

And everything from the government to the banks to Wall Street, to the colleges and the corporations they serve, gives lip service to the problem, and then gorges themselves on our blood, sweat and tears. (I told you this preface was more for the emotional crowd.)

Regardless of your income, education or where you are financially, it's time to take control of your future.

But like many people, you have serious questions that need serious, well-considered answers. Go to our website **ActandGrowRich.info**, register, log-in, and complete ACTION ALERT #1. Check off every box that applies to you.

After you've completed the book, you can take the survey again and compare it to what you took today.

ACTION ALERT #1:
TARGETING YOUR CONCERNS ABOUT
YOUR FINANCIAL FUTURE.

[ ] How do I begin saving for my, and my family's, future?
[ ] How do I know that I'm putting my money in the best place?
[ ] Will I ever earn enough to become financially independent?
[ ] Will I get to choose when I will be able to retire?
[ ] Will I be able to afford to pay for my childrens' college tuition or will they have to go into debt?
[ ] Will I ever get out of debt?
[ ] My income is necessary to run the household. If something happened to me, what would happen to my family and our plans for the future?

[ ] I've seen how devastating, emotionally and financially, long-term care can be to a family. How can I protect my family from this horrible situation?

[ ] I'm worried about my tax liability. I know taxes are going to be going up in the future. How can I protect my money from being taken by Uncle Sam? Legally, of course!

[ ] I've worked hard all my life to provide for my family. Is there any way I can protect myself financially from lawsuits, judgments, even the IRS?

Act and Grow Rich! has the answers to these questions and more.

My goals are to provide you with a clear understanding of where we have been, and how we arrived at the current crisis.

My goals are to provide you with the concepts you need to know, and the actions you need to take, to protect yourself and your family from the devastating effects of these problems. And, by taking action, you have the confidence and ability to set and achieve your goals and dreams during your retirement.

My goals are to provide you with the tools you need to help you accomplish your mission So take advantage of the **On-Line Workbooks** and **Action Alerts** throughout the book. They enhance your understanding, get you clear and focused, and can provide paths for feedback to better help you, specifically, work toward achieving your goals.

Some people believe the #1 Problem in this country is that people don't believe they can make it BIG. It's easier to be negative than positive. People give up before they really get started, because the toughest thing is to keep going. You have to have the ability to motivate yourself. You have to say, "I can do it." You have to believe that you are special: That you are worth it. And when you put action with belief, you can change your life in a short time.

Always remember these things:

1. You are responsible for your life, both good & bad
2. Excuses don't count
3. Treat people well. Truly care about others
4. Can't let others affect you negatively; make you quit on your dreams
5. Don't worry about what people say in front of you or behind your back
6. Don't worry about the things you can't control
7. You can't worry about making mistakes. You learn by trying
8. Get yourself a Mentor
9. Always be positive, excited, pumped up. It's contagious!

Looking forward to seeing how **Act & Grow Rich!** can make a difference in your life!

— **Lyle Benjamin**

FOREWORD

I am the first to admit, I wasn't the greatest student in college. School didn't hold my interest much, and I had decided early on that I didn't like working for other people much. And that included working in my family's restaurant.

I knew that being in business for myself gave me the best opportunity to make serious money. So just out of college, I started a computer company, and did pretty well. But I didn't like the fact that the products were always changing, software always needed updating, and that so much time had to spent dealing with customer issues that shouldn't have been there in the first place. I wanted a simpler model for success. I found it in real estate with its five products: residential, commercial, co-ops/condos, rentals and land.

Being in business for myself, I made it a mission to read all I could on what successful people do to reach their goals. Books like **The Power of the Subconscious Mind** to **Think and Grow Rich** to **Rich Dad, Poor Dad** to name a few.

Over the years, I spent tens of thousands of dollars attending business and self-help seminars thinking that if I got one great thing that I could successfully apply, it would be well worth the expense. And very often, I did come away with something I could use.

My success in real estate enabled me to own other businesses, restaurants, play the market, and provide for me and my family. Then a few years back I got introduced to the financial services industry by a real estate client, and got to experience first-hand the power of many of the concepts expressed in this book.

Even though I was financially in the top one percent, I never really knew how money worked, or how to build wealth tax-free. Once I saw the big picture, it was a no-brainer. I became a convert and set-up plans for myself and my family. I entered the profession, became licensed, trained, helped a lot of people, and became a mentor to others.

This book is a valuable tool that everyone should read, use and share with family, friends and organizations. It is powerful enough to change the course of people's lives in so many ways, I only wish it had been available sooner.

— **Michael Lam, CEO MD, WFG**

INTRODUCTION

As someone who has spend the majority of my life as a student in the field of finance and business, I had felt that I had received an excellent education. I studied financial theory, corporate finance, financial institutions, economics, statistics and probability, financial models and learned empirical methods of financial research.

I thought I knew everything about how money works … until I read this book, and learned how one-sided my education really was. I was only taught the Wall Street financial model. And for most people, for reasons very well explained in this book, it is a failed model.

I can only hope that the vision of the author, Lyle Benjamin, through his non-profit educational organization (www.16ThingsKidsCanDo.-Org) comes to pass. The material in this book desperately needs to be taught to high school and college students as well as the general population. Without it, we are destined to repeat the mistakes that have turned society into a class war between a small group of winners and the majority of financial losers. No disrespect intended.

In the spirit that was intended, I strongly urge you to read, understand and share **Act & Grow Rich!** with others. Only then can we effect the changes that we need in our lives and in society to put this country back on the path to equality for all.

— **Sheung Sheng, Ph.D.**

SECTION I:

**THE DECK IS STACKED, THE GAME IS RIGGED,
SO IT'S NOT OUR FAULT IF WE SUCK AT IT.**

"You cannot travel on the path until you become the path itself."
— **Gantana Bouddha**

CHAPTER 1.
WHY YOU SHOULD SPEND MORE TIME
PLANNING FOR YOUR RETIREMENT THAN YOU
SPEND GOING TO THE MOVIES.

If you ask people on the street "How long is the average movie?" most people's answer would be in the ballpark. If you ask the same people how much they really need for their retirement, they do a mighty wind up, take a big swing, and then strike out. Miserably.

The reason why is quite simple: We spend a heck of a lot more time watching movies than planning for our retirement. The fact of the matter is we spend 1,022 hours, or 42 solid days, in front of the television watching other people's lives. And that doesn't include all the time we spend watching our iPads, tablets and cell phones.

Compare that with the percentage of all Americans that have never met with a Financial Advisor. Not even once. How bad is it? Charles Schwab, the brokerage and banking company, did a survey of 1,000 of their clients: 77% had never met with a Financial Advisor.

The small percentage that do let Advisors manage their money follow the Wall Street model for building retirement. But for the vast majority of Americans, they allow their company's 401(k), organizations 403(b) or government agency's 457 plan manage their retirement.

ON-LINE WORKBOOK #1:
WHAT TYPE OF INVESTOR ARE YOU?
1. Never met with an Advisor?
2. Let your company handle it for you?
3. Have an Advisor who invests for you in the market?
4. Or research and make your own decisions?

Regardless of whether your management style is hands on or hands off, the question really boils down to this: Do you want to live your retirement years on your terms, or do you want them to, frankly, suck?

If you've invested in any of the first four areas: S&P, bonds, CDs, a house — your might have a return from 2.7% to 8.2% — but more often than not the "average investor" has the worst performance overall.

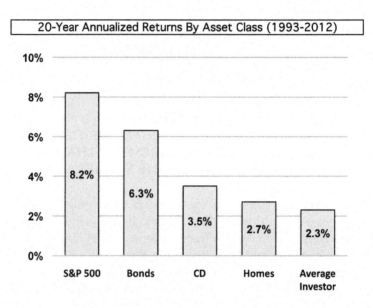

20-Year Annualized Returns By Asset Class (1993-2012)

Early in my business career, I thought people's lives could be divided into three parts: Relationships, work and sleep. I published a national newsstand magazine, "Relationships Today," that was built on the premise that too much time, energy and money is devoted to helping people get the most out of their work. There is not enough common sense education that provides us with the tools we need to develop all our relationships: Intimate, Family, Friendship and Work.

But like many people I overlooked retirement. It wasn't until many years later, after I had played the Stock Market, bought and sold investment property, did I come to understand the importance that proper retirement planning can make.

But it isn't enough to understand the need and benefits of proper planning. That's easy enough for a 10 year old to grasp when explained properly using peanut M&Ms. You need to have these four things in place to fully get it:

1. Goals
2. Concepts
3. Vehicles
4. Action

The good news is that by reading this book and doing the on-line workbooks, you'll have the first three items covered. And we can help you with #4 as well. That's actually the great news. The bad news is that it's not a sexy acronym: GCVA. None-the-less, memorize it. Follow it. Just don't try to pronounce it out loud to your family or friends. Or for that matter at work, social gatherings or any other place where more than one person congregates.

I know you're excited to get down to it, but before we get into GCVA, you should be aware of the financial context that not only sheds some light on the subject, but that can hopefully govern the path and course of your journey to achieve your goals.

So, in the context of retirement planning, we're going to take a glimpse into where we were as a country, where we are now, and what direction we're headed.

And when you have a better understanding in these areas, GCVA will be a snap for you to follow. Even if you can't pronounce it!

Read on!

"Thinking is easy, acting is difficult, and to put one's thoughts into action is the most difficult thing in the world."
— **Johann Wolfgang von Goethe**

CHAPTER 2.
FAST & FRIGHTENING FACTS.

It's true. We all know what we should be doing for our future. We all know what we need to do, even if we don't always know how to do it in ways that benefit us most. Regardless, taking action is the fundamental thing that everyone needs to do.

And how much time do we spend on doing the one thing we really need to do for our future well-being? Evidently, a lot less than we spend doing other things.

First, some no brainers:

How much time do students spend:

… getting a high school diploma?	4 years
… getting a college diploma?	4 years & 4 months
… getting a masters degree?	2.5 years
… getting a law degree?	7-9 years
… becoming a doctor?	8-12 years

Now, take a guess at some tougher ones. I put the answers afterwards, so don't peek until you guess.

How much time do women spend:

      … on their hair?

      … on shopping?

      … on losing weight?

How much time do men spend:

      … watching sports?

      … snoring?

      … passing gas?

Women spend 1.5 years on their hair! Eight years shopping! And a whopping 17 years dieting! But us men shouldn't take much comfort in these numbers. We have numbers of our own: We spend 17 years watching sports! Two years snoring! And, we pass gas 402,000 times during our lives. And no I'm not going to crunch the numbers on how much time this is!

Yes. Now you know the truth. No matter how ridiculous it seems, we men spend more time passing gas in elevators, than we do planning our retirements.

How much time do people spend:

... watching TV?	42 days/year
... working on their tax return?	13 hours

How much time do people spend planning their:

... wedding?	36 Days
... vacation?	20-25+ hours
... doing research on what car to buy?	10 hours

AND NOW "THE MILLION DOLLAR" QUESTION ...

HOW MUCH TIME DO PEOPLE SPEND
PLANNING THEIR RETIREMENT?

LESS THAN 5 HOURS A YEAR!
LESS TIME THAN THEY SPEND IN THE MOVIE THEATRE!

As far the saying goes, "Houston, I think we have a problem," let me add the following: "America, I think this is a major source of the problem." Read on!

"The only thing that interferes with my learning is my education."
— **Albert Einstein**

CHAPTER 3.
THE FAILURE OF OUR INSTITUTIONS:
THE BIG LIE & THE SECRET WHY.

The big lie is everywhere around us. We hear it from our parents and grandparents as we grow up. We hear it from our teachers more and more often as we progress up the ladder towards high school graduation. Even our college educational system, in some form or fashion, is built on this lie.

Go to school. Work hard. Get an education. Get a good job. Work hard. Get promotions. Get a better paying job. And everything will work out great. You'll become part of the American Dream. You'll be set for life. Get a good education, and you're set. Sound familiar?

Do you know how many millions of people walked this path and ended up running down a long, hard road only to find their golden years filled with broken promises, stress and more years of hard labor?

And the floodgates are just beginning to open. Here come the Baby Boomers, a huge number of people born after World War II, and the vast majority of them are marching off the financial cliff never able to find the promised land during their retirement.

If you're younger than Boomers, part of the Generation X, you're next in line to go through the same cycle. History repeats itself. A pretty smart individual once said that the definition of insanity is doing the same thing over and over and expecting different results.

So you can't depend on your family for expert advice because that's like the blind leading the blind. They are a product of the same system you are. And the system is fundamentally flawed.

You can't depend on our educational system for help with properly building for your future. They are into either making money at the expense of their students and in bed with the enemy: corporations.

First things first. There are so many systemic problems in higher education it would take several books just to cover the basics. Instead, see if these things ring true:

Schools provide majors with the lure of students finding good paying jobs in those majors when they graduate. True or false? Then why do so many schools push majors and curriculum when both the demand and the pay aren't great? (i.e. Computer Networking when any 12 year old with a smartphone and a tablet knows how to do it?)

Have you or someone you know, ever tried to transfer from one school to another? See if this sounds about right: The incoming school has disapproved half of the previous schools credits, and now you have to take the courses over again. Can you say "ka-ching?"

How about on-line educational courses? Great way to save both the university and students time, energy and money, right? Well, half right. The school saves money on the costs associated with classrooms, and gets to enroll a larger number of students than an ordinary course. So on-line classes should cost less, right? Nope. Students pay the same regardless of cost savings and higher revenue for the school.

Now, let's examine it from a different perspective. You go to school for 12, 16, 20, 22, 24 years or more, and what do you learn how to do? Produce a single sheet of paper called a resume that is designed to get you a job … a job that will control and govern all aspects of your life for years and years to come.

In short, your education gives you the tools you need to earn money. But what is missing? The education you need to understand how money really works. And the tools you need to manage your money to get it work hard for you. Putting it in the bank and earning 0% interest is not getting your money to work hard for you.

And for you smart-alecs out there who are indignantly thinking, "I would never think that putting my money in the bank is an investment. I have a financial adviser and I put my money in the market!" Well, that might not be the smartest place either when you consider it's subject to taxation and loss. But more on that later. Much more.

There are many reasons that factor into "The Why" of "The Big Lie." But what they all boil down to is money. Schools teach what companies want them to teach. If there were no company jobs at the end of the rainbow, the schools wouldn't be able to tout their job placement success rates. Less students would take those courses, and the school wouldn't make as much money. And, of course, even non-profit schools are all about making money.

But that's not the only reason. Banks and Wall Street make a lot of money off of people that don't know how money works (and how to get it work hard for them). And, I promise, more on that too.

Just keep this in mind. Only four states require a basic course in financial literacy during high school. 33 states and the District of Columbia require sex education/instruction about HIV/AIDS. And 29 states have driver's education. And it doesn't get better in college or graduate school.

I have been mentoring college students from major universities for years through my non-profit education organization's internship, work experience and career track program, and even when students major in finance, economics and business – they do not learn the most important rules that govern building wealth (other than the time/value relationship of money).

Without exception, what they learn is the Wall Street model of building wealth. And that is playing the Stock Market. Don't be fooled by people that say they earned money in the market. For the vast majority of players, it's no different than gambling. You choose your stocks and then you pray you have some luck. And like Willie Nelson sings, "You got to know when to hold them. Know when to fold them." And know when to walk away because it just ain't worth the risk.

So don't you think there is something fundamentally wrong with our educational system when it isn't even willing to teach its students the basic financial strategies they need to have a fighting chance at managing thier money properly?

Still not convinced?

Read on!

"Things remain the same because it is impossible to change very much without changing most of everything."
— **Ted Sizer, Educator and Author**

CHAPTER 4.
LIVING IN THE 51ST STATE: THE STATE OF DENIAL.

Remember this? "The definition of insanity is doing the same thing over and over again and then expecting different results." Well, the person that coined the phrase was none-other than Mr. Einstein. And doing the same thing over and over again, and failing is fine if you're playing competitive sports where every season you reset to zero and hope for a championship.

But if you're working for your financial future, it sucks as a game plan.

Putting your money, over and over again, into the bank for savings or into a retirement plan like a 401(k), 403(b), 457 plan each paycheck … is not the best way to save for your retirement. Not by a long shot.

Don't believe me?

"Overall, 76% (of survey respondents) said they always or usually live paycheck to paycheck..." according to a **CNNMoney.com** survey.

45% of workers have no retirement savings. Yet, retirees typically need to have 75% to 80% of their annual income to keep up their lifestyle. That's 75% to 80% year after year after year.

If your annual income was $50,000 before retirement, you would need $37,500 to $40,000 per year to live on. Now multiply this figure by the number of years you plan on living. Retire at 65 and you'll need almost $1,000,000 over the next 30 years to live. Cheaply, of course.

And by the way, that doesn't take into account the high costs of both TAXATION and INFLATION on your money!

Run your own numbers and see how you're doing. I know it might be depressing. But if you've like most people, you've got to get slapped around a bit before you get motivated enough to get your backside off the sofa and do something about it.

ACTION ALERT #2:
YOUR OWN RETIREMENT CALCULATOR

But the dismal financial numbers is only one side of the coin, so to speak. On the other side is the American Dream: A dream that has been slowly turning into a nightmare for millions and millions of us.

Read on, if you dare.

"90% of the people in the stock market, professionals and amateurs alike, simply haven't done enough homework."
— **William J. O'Neil**

CHAPTER 5.
THE DEATH OF THE AMERICAN DREAM.

Many moons ago (1931 to be exact) author James Truslow Adams wrote the book, "The Epic of America." In it, he stated the American Dream is where "life should be better and richer and fuller for everyone, with opportunity for each according to ability or achievement … each man and each woman shall be able to attain the fullest stature of which they are innately capable, and be recognized by others for what they are, regardless of the fortuitous circumstances of birth or position."

And for the next 40 or 50 years America seemed to be working hard to improve and live up to that ideal. After World War II, American soldiers came home from the war, and in addition to making babies in record numbers, went to college in record numbers.

Whole industries developed and prospered because of the rise of the Baby Boomers – from baby food to diapers to toys to bicycles to cars to college education to home ownership.

The stock market was slowly but steadily climbing in seemingly a never ending upward progression. Families funded their homes, their children's education and their retirement on their stock market portfolio, their pensions, their social security benefits and their savings.

For the post World War II generation, the 76 million Baby Boomers and their children, Generation X, there was no end in sight to continued prosperity. Your company, the government and the Market would take care of you from retirement till you died.

And that usually came 5 to 10 years later, leaving your surviving spouse and children with a small inheritance. It was a great system.

But then two things happened that not only changed the system, they broke it.

During the first 10 years of the new Millennium the Stock Market suf-

Lyle Benjamin

fered two declines that devastated investors. In 2001, the Market tanked by 50% while the NASDAQ lost a staggering 80% of its valuation by 2002! And then in 2008, the bottom fell out again as the Market crashed with another 50% drop!

People that were counting on this money for their retirement were crushed as their portfolios lost half their value.

Imagine saving up for 30 to 40 years, and expecting to have enough money to live out the next 15 to 20 years in comfort. Then, suddenly, 10 years of your dream lifestyle are wiped away in a flash. You'd want to hang your head and cry. And a lot of people did for a long time.

And if you think you can time the market and get out ahead of the avalanche, trying to time the market is next to impossible: You never know when disaster is going to strike, or how long it's going to last.

S&P Largest Daily Point Losses				
Rank	Date	Close	Net Change	% Change
1	Sep. 29, 2008	1,106.42	-106.85	-8.81
2	Oct. 15, 2008	907.84	-90.17	-9.03
3	Apr. 14, 2000	1,356.56	-83.95	-5.83
4	Dec. 1, 2008	816.21	-80.03	-8.93
5	Aug. 8, 2011	1,119.46	-79.92	-6.66
6	Aug. 24, 2015	1,893.21	-77.68	-3.94
7	Oct. 9, 2008	909.92	-75.02	-7.62
8	Aug. 31, 1998	957.28	-69.86	-6.80
9	Aug. 21, 2015	1,970.89	-64.84	-3.19
10	Oct. 27, 1997	876.99	-64.65	-6.87

20 Out Of 20 Of The Largest Daily Losses Have Occurred Since 1987

Now, the second thing that changed the course of retirement came in the form of good news. Better healthcare, nutrition and fitness added up to a longer life expectancy.

US Life Expectancy Table	
Year	Age
1960	69.77
1970	70.81
1980	73.66
1990	75.22
2000	76.64
2010	78.54

If you were 65 years old in 1960, you were expected kick the bucket less than five years later. By 1980, life expectancy was stretched to almost nine years. And by 2010, people were expected to live 14 years past the retirement age of 65.

For a baby born today, some estimates of life expectancy reach upwards of 120 years! That's really amazing.

Unfortunately, living longer spelled disaster for people's retirement. Harris International did a survey of adults between 45 and 65. 66% of the people were more afraid of outliving their money than they were about dying too young.

And it's completely understandable. Take a few minutes and visualize one or two of your retirement goals and dreams. Laying on the sand on a tropical beach sipping Margaritas? Traveling Europe by car or rail? Going out on the water on your own boat?

Now, imagine talking to your kids about running out of money and needing to sell the house where they grew up. Or having to go back to work, but not having the health, skills or desire to deal with the rat race.

Do you know who the two biggest employers are of people over 60 years old in this country? Walmart and McDonalds. Together they employ over 1,800,000 people in the United States with Walmart coming in at #1 with 1.4 million and McDonalds at #3 with 440,000.

Don't want to work? Can't find a good job? Now imagine having to move in with your kids because they need to support you. Not a pretty picture. But this could be your life in retirement.

Still not convinced?

Read on!

"Rise early, work hard, strike oil."
— J Paul Getty

CHAPTER 6.
THE FORCED RETIREMENT OF THE
OLD SCHOOL RETIREMENT MODEL.

For much of the 20th century, industries were flush with money and companies rewarded employees with the promise of prosperity in retirement through what became know as "The Three-Legged Stool" model: People were able to build for retirement through the combination of pensions, Social Security and savings.

The Three-Legged Stool of Retirement

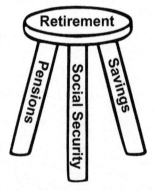

The fact that many people worked hard for 40 years, retired and then dropped dead within five years helped the system run smoothly. Cracks in the stool started to develop when advances in medicine, nutrition, and physical fitness expanded people's life expectancy longer and longer.

The longer people lived past their employment, the thinner their savings became. Think of spreading mayonnaise on a long submarine sandwich. You start at one end with a large dollop and as you spread it gets thinner and thinner. This is what happens to your savings if you live too long, eventually you'll use it up and it runs out.

Pensions were established to reward people for loyal service to the company by providing them with a percentage of their income from the time they retired to the time they died. And that was a great way for companies to lock in their employees for a lifetime of service: A pot of cash at the end of a lifetime of labor. And it worked very well. For a time. When companies started to see more and more people living 10, 15, 20 years after they retired, their accountants crunched the numbers. And crapped in their pants (figuratively we hope).

Funding the pension plans for longer and longer times started to eat into company profits. And it had a domino effect. American companies felt they couldn't compete on prices against Europeans because the high cost of their pensions drove up the prices they had to charge for goods.

Private-sector based pensions went from protecting the Golden Years of over 30 million workers — 45% of the workforce — in 1979 to less than 13% by 2010.

And make no mistake, where pensions still exist, companies and governments, both large and small, have been working hard at reducing the benefits to employees. The Governor of New Jersey, Chris Christy, has been embroiled in multiple lawsuits after both underfunding the state's pension plan, and diverting pension cash to fund other programs.

Unfortunately, the final leg in the stool, Social Security, isn't going to provide much comfort either. Social Security started as a noble enterprise in 1935 to provide "for the material needs of individuals and families; To protect aged and disabled persons against the expenses of illnesses that may otherwise use up their savings; To keep families together; and to give children the chance to grow up healthy and secure."

When people first started drawing benefits there were 45 workers contributing to every one person receiving benefits. Care to guess what that ratio is today? 100 to 1? 50 to 1? 25 to 1? 15 to 1? 10 to 1? How about 2.8 to 1? Yep. And that figure is a large part of the reason why Social Security is not sustainable: Not enough people paying in compared to how much is going out.

The second reason why Social Security is only So-So Security is the same problem that led to the demise of pensions: People are living much longer. The system wasn't really designed to have people take out for almost as long as they paid in. It worked great when people paid in for 40 years and then took out for 5 or 10. Not so well when people take out for 20 or 30 years.

So how do you think the government is going to "fix" the problem?

One easy way is to tack on more years before people can start taking benefits. Move the early eligibility age to 67, and the full benefits age to 75. And go even longer for younger workers: Early at 72. Full at 80. And for the Next Generation? Go boldly where no one has gone before: Early at 80. Full at 90.

If that doesn't make your stomach churn, don't worry, I'm not done yet. Lets say the current monthly cash benefits you can receive are thus: Early at 62 = $1,200. Full at 66 = $1,600. Currently the system allows for Automatic Cost-of-Living Adjustments (COLAs) that are tied to ... well, something.

Automatic Cost-Of-Living-Adjustments			
1975	8.0%	1996	2.6%
1976	6.4%	1997	2.9%
1977	5.9%	1998	2.1%
1978	6.5%	1999	1.3%
1979	9.9%	2000	2.5%
1980	14.3%	2001	3.5%
1981	11.2%	2002	2.6%
1982	7.4%	2003	1.4%
1984	3.5%	2004	2.1%
1985	3.5%	2005	2.7%
1986	3.1%	2006	4.1%
1987	1.3%	2007	3.3%
1988	4.2%	2008	2.3%
1989	4.0%	2009	5.8%
1990	4.7%	2010	0.0%
1991	5.4%	2011	0.0%
1992	3.7%	2012	3.6%
1993	3.0%	2013	1.7%
1994	2.6%	2014	1.5%
1995	2.8%	2015	1.7%

I don't know about you, but I'm pretty sure the cost of some necessities went up by more than 'zero' in 2010-11. And if you look at the numbers they seem to be going down in a pretty consistent pattern over the years.

If I were a *betting man, I'm going to take an educated guess that the "Powers That Be" are going to flat line the COLA benefits somewhere down the line.

*FYI: I'm not. I gave that up when I stopped trying to win money in the stock market. And, before the emails start coming in, I've never bought a lottery ticket in my life, either. I think the system is flawed. Instead of giving $250 million to one or two winners, divide the pot progressively and spread the wealth to a much larger number of people!

The reason for taking away people's COLA? It keeps more money in the system and prolongs the life of the patient. And although that might sound like a good plan, think about it this way: How would you like to get $3,000 a month in benefits in the year 2030? And then get that same $3,000 per year in the year 2045?

Ever hear about inflation? Well, the definition goes like this: "The rate at which the general level of prices for goods and services is rising, and, subsequently, purchasing power is falling."

What this means is that when you go to pay your rent in year 2045, if you haven't planned properly for your retirement, you may be living in your grandkids basement because that's all you can afford.

But just to make sure you get the point that Social Security is not going to be your salvation, let's add a few more nails to its coffin. How would you feel if you paid into the SS System for 40 or 50 years, and then the "Powers That Be" decided to:

1. Tax your SS benefits?

2. Cut your benefits because you have other income or assets?

3. Eliminate your benefits because you have other assets?

Sucks right? Well, the sooner you face up the truth of the matter – that So So Security will be D.O.A. for millions of people in the future, and chances are you're one of them – the sooner you can start doing something about it.

And by doing something about it, I don't mean writing your Congressperson or stop paying into the System. The former is like shouting to Mount Olympus and expecting something to happen. Not. The latter is just going to piss off your Uncle Sam. And you don't want to do that unless you want free room and board in The Big House (AKA the Slammer in case you didn't know).

And now that we are on a roll with bad news, let's keep it going with some truly distressing news.

Read on!

"Models work when they are appropriate for the particular circumstance, but some of the best investment judgments over time have come when people recognized that models derived in other periods were broken or not directly relevant."
– **Abby Joseph Cohen**

CHAPTER 7.
THE BUST OF OUR 401(k), 403(b), 457 DEFINED COMPENSATION RETIREMENT BENEFITS PLANS.

In the early 1980s when more and more companies wanted to retire their pension and thrift plans because of their high expenses, large companies (Johnson & Johnson, PepsiCo, JC Penney, Honeywell, Savannah Foods & Industries and Hughes Aircraft Company) replaced them with plans derived from section 401(k) of the Internal Revenue Code.

This code allowed employees to contribute part of their pre-tax wages into managed retirement plans and receive a tax-deferment until withdrawn at retirement age. Companies were allowed to set up a percentage based matching program to sweeten the pot and encourage employees to participate.

On the surface these retirement plans were a win, win, win.

Winner #1: Companies got to scrap their high cost pension plans matching a small percentage that kicked in only if the employee contributed a like amount to their retirement. But the best part was that all company contributions ended when employment ended. Pensions had companies on the hook for 30%, 50%, 70% of an employee's annual salary until the former employee passed. Paying a small matching percentage into a 401(k) plan for 10, 15 or 20 years amounted to what the company would have had to pay out of a pension for a year or two.

From 1981 to 2012 the number of companies offering 401(k) plans grew from essentially nothing to over 515,000 with over 52 millions American workers participating to the tune of 2.8 trillion dollars. Can you whistle loudly?

By comparison, mutual fund assets held in retirement accounts (IRAs and Defined Contribution plans including 401(k) plans) stood at $6.8

trillion as of June 30, 2014, or 43 percent of overall mutual fund assets according to a recent report from the Investment Company Institute.

Winner #2: Wall Street. Do you think it's a coincidence that the stock market rose only 100 points from 1950 to 1979, and then with the introduction of the 401(k), went up like a rocket? From 1980 to 2015 the S&P rose over 2,000 points as the number of investment dollars went from $1.5 trillion to over $21 trillion! At the same time the Dow went from approximately 1,000 points to over 18,000!

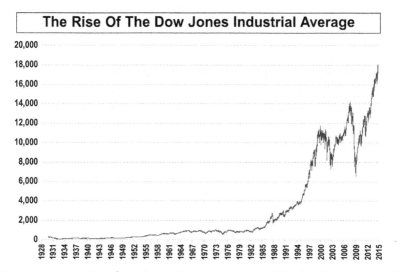

Investment banker, hedge fund manager, securities broker became the hottest jobs on the planet.

And who makes the commissions? Wall Street.

And who manages the funds? Wall Street.

And who receives their commissions, regardless of performance? Wall Street.

And who paid out millions in bonuses even when Americans were going bankrupt in record numbers? Wall Street.

Point to remember: You don't earn money in the Stock Market. You win it. Or you lose it.

And you can't influence the outcome by working hard. You can't predict the outcome by following trends. You can't time the market. In short, you're taking a risk by just being in the game.

At best, it's an educated gamble. At worst, it's a free falling nightmare into a black pit that smothers your dreams in ashes.

And from my experience and perspective, the only people that should take the risk – are people that can afford to lose the money. And that's not most of us.

Winner #3: Uncle Sam. How does the government come out of this a winner? Well, remember that tax deferment you received when you put your money into a 401(k)? The one you were so happy and eager to get? Fast forward to age 65. You just had your retirement party. You plan on kicking back and traveling around the globe. One new country a year! Shorter trips around the good 'ole US of A. Sounds like a dream come true!

Your plan is to take out $40,000 a year from your 401(k) account, but you forgot one small detail ... it's time to pay the piper. It's tax time. And when you need the money the most (and you're not working) you're going to have to pay 25%, 30%, 35%, 40%, maybe even 50% to the government.

Here's the deal. The government was very smart. You could have paid 30% in taxes ($1,500) on the $5,000 you put in your 401(k) plan back in 1998. Instead, you elected to get the deferment and wait until it was time to harvest your crop before you had to pay your tax bill.

Now, 30 years later your $5,000 increased to $50,000 and your tax bill went up along with it. I don't know about you, but I'd rather pay the $1,500 now, not the $15,000, $20,000 or $30,000 later.

Remember, this was a win, win, win scenario? Sounded great right? But we still have one more participant to add to the equation.

Loser #1: Us. Our retirement is now largely in the hands of Wall Street. Companies are fine with this because of the savings to their bottom line. For the company, it doesn't matter how your retirement funds perform: It's not their problem. They gave us the freedom to sign-in, make choices, and they even contribute additional cash in the form of a match. In their eyes, they are the hero.

But the truth of the matter is that large companies no longer have loyalty to short, medium or long-term employees. Their major focus is how they appeal to Wall Street. Anything and everything they can do to improve their "financial image" is seemingly fair game. And that includes everything from cutting employee benefits to cutting employees.

I have an associate, Andy, who worked for IBM for twenty years. He managed a team of 144 programmers. One day his boss calls him into his office. Half expecting a raise, he's told instead to look for another job. Andy, who took the job with IBM out of college because of their policy "IBM for Life" goes home and cries. He manages to transfer to another department and save his job, but IBM lays off over a thousand employees.

And, as you might know, this isn't unusual. Many workers devote years and years to their companies putting up with everything from low wages and high taxes to unsatisfactory working conditions, unful-filling work, unhappy bosses, unhappy co-workers and stressful com-mutes. And why do they do it? "It pays the bills."

But the hope that people can pay their bills, live comfortably, and build up enough for their future is beyond the sights of too many work-ing class people. And for the ones that think they are doing enough to build for their future … ?

Well, this is what Time magazine said about investing in your 401(k). "The ugly truth, though, is that the 401(k) is a lousy idea, a financial flop, a rotten repository for our retirement reserves."

Forbes magazine had this to say, "A 55-year-old employed man who wanted to withdraw $50,000 from his 401(k) would get to keep only $32,500 because $17,500 would go to taxes and the early-withdrawal penalty."

But one of the biggest slams came in the form of an investigative piece done by award-winning CBS journalism television show, **60 Minutes,** where they characterized it as "... a retirement system that's jeopardized the financial security of tens of millions of people."

ACTION ALERT #3:
SINGING THE RETIREMENT PLAN BLUES.

We'd like to hear from you and see what you have to say on the sub-ject. Any personal experience you'd care to share? Simply log-in and submit.

But now that we've explored how miserable, deplorable and shock-ingly ineffective retirement plans are for most of us, you're going to learn that's not even the bad news. It gets worse. Much worse.

Read on!

"First weigh the considerations, then take the risks."
— **Helmuth von Moltke**

CHAPTER 8.
WALL STREET'S DIRTY SECRET:
THE EFFECTS OF MARKET LOSS ON YOUR MONEY.

Taxes are not the only issue you have to contend with when investing in the market. Another factor that keeps investors up at night is market volatility leading to market losses.

There is a dirty little secret that Wall Street is allowed to do to fool investors into thinking that all is well in the land of the bull. (Pun intended.)

Let's say you owned a stock and one year it gained 10% and then the following year it lost 10%. And over the next 10 years the stock repeated this pattern of up 10% and down 10%. And the end of this period, the stock had five years of 10% gain followed by five years of 10% loss.

That means that gains were canceled out by losses and you had a 0% return on your investment. Right? Absolutely right, if you work on Wall Street.

100% wrong if you do the math. Look at the graph. Based on a starting figure of $10,000 dollars you would lose $490 by the end of the 10-year period.

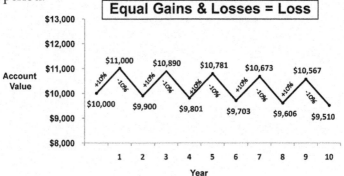

As usual, what you don't know CAN HURT YOU! Look at what market loss can do to your money, and then look at what you would have to gain just to break even again:

The Effect Of Loss On Investments:						
			Gain:			
Example 1:	$1,000	-	10%	=		$900
Investment: $1,000	$900	+	10%	=		$990
Market Loss: - 10%	$900	+	11%	=		$1,000
Example 2:	$20,000	-	20%	=		$16,000
Investment: $20,000	$16,000	+	20%	=		$19,200
Market Loss: - 20%	$16,000	+	25%	=		$20,000
Example 3:	$50,000	-	30%	=		$35,000
Investment: $50,000	$35,000	+	30%	=		$45,500
Market Loss: - 30%	$35,000	+	43%	=		$50,000
Example 4:	$100,000	-	40%	=		$60,000
Investment: $100,000	$60,000	+	40%	=		$84,000
Market Loss: - 40%	$60,000	+	67%	=		$100,000
Example 4:	$200,000	-	50%	=		$100,000
Investment: $200,000	$100,000	+	50%	=		$150,000
Market Loss: - 50%	$100,000	+	100%	=		$200,000

Lose 30% and you have to gain 43% just to break even.

Lose 40% and you have to gain 67% just to break even.

Lose 50% and you have to gain 100% just to break even.

Let me you a question. How often have you seen stocks doubling after taking huge losses? Not often I bet.

And how many times has the market tanked by double digits in the last 30 years? Five times! Just about once every few years: 1987, 1991, 1998, 2001, 2008.

If you think that one-day market drops are the financial equivalent of going to the amusement park and taking the ride that goes straight up and then drops you straight down leaving your stomach still at the top where you started ... Then this next table is the same as taking the roller coaster ride from financial hell.

Oops! Wrong image. Here's the table:

Market Loss During Recession			
Name:	Year(s):	S&P 500 Loss:	Dow Market Loss:
Housing Bubble	2008-2009	56.40%	Dropped 50%
Dot-Com Bubble	2001	49.10%	Dopped 38%
Recession	1990-1991	14.00%	Dropped 18%
Stock Market Crash	1987	33.50%	Fell 22.6%
Recession	1980-1982	27.80%	Dropped 22.6%
Recession	1973-1975	48.00%	Dropped 45%
Recession	1970	36.10%	Dropped 30%
Crash	1966	22.20%	
Cuban Missile Crisis	1962	28.00%	Dropped 26.5%
Recession	1960		Dropped 13.9%
Recession	1957	20.70%	Dropped 14.1%
Recession	1950-1953		Dropped 11%
Recession	1949	29.60%	Dropped 19.3%
Recession	1945		Fell 19.3%
Great Recession	1929	86.10%	Fell 90%

And like I said previously, you never know when it's going to happen. It might take only a matter of weeks to drop that much. But when it does, it might take your portfolio years to recover.

Unfortunately, a 50% drop isn't the worst of it. I've had stocks lose 99.9% of their value! Those babies are never coming back! And, if I knew then what I know now, I never would have done my investing the same way.

A wise man by the name of Warren Buffett once said that the number one rule of investing is "never lose money." Too bad his next tip wasn't putting people on the right path to follow his advice. Read on!

"In this world nothing can be certain, except death and taxes."
— **Benjamin Franklin**

CHAPTER 9.
THE BIGGEST CHECK YOU DON'T WANT TO
GET AT RETIREMENT ... ?

U.S. debt is 18 trillion and each American – including newborn babies – are responsible for $154,000 of it.

That's over $150,000 in debt for every man, woman and child in the United States. And if you think that's bad, it gets worse. Much worse.

If you have a business and you acquire debt, Uncle Sam requires that you add up all the future obligations you're on the hook for, and put that on the books starting at year one. For example, Company X buys a very large copy machine with payments of $100,000 due per year over the next five years. The total obligation of $500,000 has to be shown on the books in the year it was acquired.

Simple right? Not exactly.

The government doesn't want to drive people to drink, so they use a different accounting method to calculate government debt in order to make the figure more palatable. Let's say the government is on the hook for some military funding to the tune of $500,000,000 over the next five years.

Ordinarily, that $500 million would have to go on the books at the time the debt was incurred. The same would be true for our educational obligations, medical obligations, infrastructure obligations, administrative obligations, loan obligations, etc.

After we add up all those government "000000s" the amount of U.S. debt is actually over 80 trillion dollars! But it's only because of some sleight of hand that the government is able to take advantage of accounting methods not available to the rest of us.

This way, Uncle Sam is able to drop the "debt" figure to show only the money that it's required to pay out each year. And currently, that's the lesser of the two evils ... the 18 trillion.

Now, the government doesn't have to show the real figure of 80 trillion, it can bury the $684,376 for every man, woman and child in this country. Or the $1,200,000 in debt for every working stiff in the country.

ACTION ALERT #4:
CHECK OUT WWW.USDEBTCLOCK.ORG

Check out the numbers. It's pretty scary stuff, but watching the numbers tick up is way cool!

Okay! Enough with the numbers. What's this all really mean? Well, debts are financial obligations. Obligations have to be paid back. The money to pay them back has to come from somewhere. That somewhere is really someone. That someone is really us. And because us elected the government to represent us, that us is able to charge this us — are you ready for it? — TAXES to pay the debts that that us got this us into.

Get it? Got it! Good.

Now, let me ask you a very important question. Knowing what you now know about our debt, do you think taxes are going to go up, down or stay the same in the future? My bet is on "up."

But it's not just because of the $654,000 per person we're currently on the hook for. Think about the future costs in these three areas:

    1. climate change
    2. infrastructure repair
    3. medical costs

I watch "ABC World News Tonight" and every night for past year there has been at least 5 to 10 minutes of news each show on weather conditions that are putting tens of millions of people at risk on a daily basis.

In just the past year there has been a record amount of snowfall in many parts of the country. And a record number of recorded tornadoes. Record rainfalls. Record flooding. Record earthquakes. Record heat levels. Record forest fires.

Who pays for all this damage? We do in the form of our tax dollars. And if you think paying for this type of damage is costly, how about paying for preventative measures? Now factor in the cost of stopping rising ocean levels from drowning New York, L.A. and Miami, just to name a few coastal cities. The costs are going to be off the charts. And who pays for all that prevention? We do. In the form of our tax dollars.

What are the estimates on the costs associated with storm damage?

What are the estimates on the costs associated with protecting cities?

What are the estimates on the costs associated with repairing our crumbling infrastructure of bridges, roads and dams?

The fact is we don't know the answers to these questions. Or at least, we're not being made privy to the estimates. Regardless, the numbers are going to be astronomical, that much is certain.

But many economists believe that the biggest threat to our country, financially speaking, is going to be the high cost of Medicare and Medicaid. Already it is consuming over 20% of GDP.

Now here's the kicker. Do you realize that our current tax rate of 39.6% is a full 50 points lower than the top rate American's have paid in the past? Look at the graph, and see for yourself.

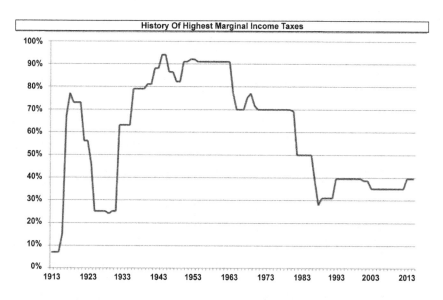

From 1950 to 1963, the tax rate in this country topped 90% for people earning over $100,000 per year!

So you tell me. Do you think your taxes are likely to be going up? Down? Or stay the same in the future?

ACTION ALERT #5:
THE HIGH COST OF TAXES.

Share your thoughts on the high cost of taxes. Log-in and speak up! And when the time comes for you to act on what you're learning, I just may have saved you from getting the biggest check you never wanted to get at retirement — A REALITY CHECK — in the form of 40%, 50%, 60%, 70% taxes!

Understanding the ramifications of taxation so important I'd like you to take a look at the tax data again, this time as a table:

Historical Highest Marginal Income Tax Rates (1913-2015)							
Year	Top Marginal		Year	Top Marginal		Year	Top Marginal
1913	7.0%		1948	82.1%		1983	50.0%
1914	7.0%		1949	82.1%		1984	50.0%
1915	7.0%		1950	91.0%		1985	50.0%
1916	15.0%		1951	91.0%		1986	50.0%
1917	67.0%		1952	92.0%		1987	38.5%
1918	77.0%		1953	92.0%		1988	28.0%
1919	73.0%		1954	91.0%		1989	31.0%
1920	73.0%		1955	91.0%		1990	31.0%
1921	73.0%		1956	91.0%		1991	31.0%
1922	56.0%		1957	91.0%		1992	31.0%
1923	56.0%		1958	91.0%		1993	39.6%
1924	46.0%		1959	91.0%		1994	39.6%
1925	25.0%		1960	91.0%		1995	39.6%
1926	25.0%		1961	91.0%		1996	39.6%
1927	25.0%		1962	91.0%		1997	39.6%
1928	25.0%		1963	91.0%		1998	39.6%
1929	24.0%		1964	77.0%		1999	39.6%
1930	25.0%		1965	70.0%		2000	39.6%
1931	25.0%		1966	70.0%		2001	38.6%
1932	63.0%		1967	70.0%		2002	38.6%
1933	63.0%		1968	75.3%		2003	35.0%
1934	63.0%		1969	77.0%		2004	35.0%
1935	63.0%		1970	71.8%		2005	35.0%
1936	79.0%		1971	70.0%		2006	35.0%
1937	79.0%		1972	70.0%		2007	35.0%
1938	79.0%		1973	70.0%		2008	35.0%
1939	79.0%		1974	70.0%		2009	35.0%
1940	81.1%		1975	70.0%		2010	35.0%
1941	81.0%		1976	70.0%		2011	35.0%
1942	88.0%		1977	70.0%		2012	35.0%
1943	88.0%		1978	70.0%		2013	39.6%
1944	94.0%		1979	70.0%		2014	39.6%
1945	94.0%		1980	70.0%		2015	39.6%
1946	86.5%		1981	69.1%		Tax Rate 50% or More:	
1947	86.5%		1982	50.0%		62 Years	

Remember though, the time to act and protect yourself from taxation is now! Not down the road when it may be too late.
Read on!

"He who will not economize will have to agonize."
— **Confucius**

CHAPTER 10.
THE BIG ZERO: HOW WE SPEND OUR MONEY.

Time to be proactive! Please get out a pen and piece of paper. You can do this along with me without going online.

ACTION ALERT #6:
THE BIG ZERO.

If I were to draw a pie chart to show how people spend the money they make during the month, it would look something like this. Draw a circle in the center. Next draw a vertical line down the middle of the circle to divide it in two halves.

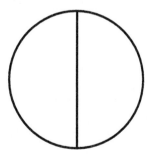

On the right half of the circle write the words LIVING EXPENSES. About 50% of everything you make goes toward your living expenses. Your rent, your utilities and your food. All the basic necessities required to live. And in places like New York, your living expenses can run a lot more than 50% of your income.

Now draw a horizontal line through the middle of the remaining half circle. Add the word DEBT because another big portion of what you pay out each month goes to pay for good old-fashioned debt. We don't

do a lot of manufacturing in this country anymore, but we do manufac-
ture a lot of debt. We have become a society of consumers, not a society of savers.

And so, here is another huge problem in America: Debt is a huge
plague on our society. And it doesn't matter if you make $2,000 a month
or $20,000 a month. Whatever you make your debt level is going to rise
concurrently. If you're making $20,000 a month are you going to live in
the same apartment or neighborhood you did when you earned $2,000
a month? Probably not. Are you going to eat at the same restaurants?
Are you going to take the same vacations? Are you going to drive the
same car? Probably not. Probably not. Probably not. Heck you might
not even have the same friends any more!

I believe that we are not able to save money because we are drowning
in debt. According to CCN Money.com, the Average American family
carries $10,000 to $16,000 in credit card debt.

Many people figure "What's the point?" They hope to start saving
once they dig themselves out of their hole. But the problem is that your
debt is constantly working against you. Every night when you go to
sleep, it's working against you. Every day when you get up, it's working against you. It costs us billions upon billions of dollars in not only
interest and fees, but also in the high cost of stress, depression and broken marriages.

On the remaining section of the pie chart, add the word TAXES to the
bottom section. This is the portion of your money that goes to Uncle
Sam. You know, the government doesn't trust you, and when you earn
money, they take your taxes out in advance. But it's not just that you
pay taxes on what you earn. There are hidden taxes on what you spend
your money on too. You have a cell phone? There are taxes built right
into your bill. You have cable tv? Hidden taxes. Own a car and pump
gas? Same thing. Then when you go shopping and buy things, their are
the obvious taxes added right onto your bill.

Now, try to save some money in the bank and guess what? The government taxes that too. And it doesn't matter whether you earned $5 in
interest or $5,000, Uncle Sam wants his slice. And he gets it through a
little slip of paper called a 1099-DIV form you have to fill with your tax
return.

Here's where we are now:
> You **EARN** money and ..... Uncle Sam **TAXES** you.
> You **SPEND** money and ... Uncle Sam **TAXES** you.
> You **SAVE** money and ...... Uncle Sam **TAXES** you.

Then, you live a good long life and you want to leave a legacy behind
for your children or grandchildren, and Uncle Sam is going to tax that

too. It's called Estate Taxes, and as of today, the tax rate is at 55%. And if your estate doesn't have the cash to pay your tax bill, the assets that you wanted to pass on are going to get liquified. Then after all the taxes are paid, you children or grandkids will still have to pay inheritance taxes on what they receive.

Then you **DIE** and .... Uncle Sam **TAXES** you. Again.

If you're paying attention, you can now see how much of your hard-earned money is going to feed the government.

When you add it all up, taxes are going to be the biggest problem that prevents you from becoming financially independent during your lifetime.

Now raise your hand if you think taxes are going up in the future. In case you can't see it, both my hands are in the air. Don't get me wrong. I am all for paying my fair share of taxes for government services like police, firemen, education, bridges and roads, and all these things. But I don't like paying my unfair share, do you? Nope? Well, we'll get into that a little later.

So here is what the circle looks like for most people:

But if you want to be financially independent, what is missing in how you allocate your money every month? The answer is the part that goes to your savings or investments. Basically, your retirement plan.

And you know what? In this country we have one of the lowest savings rates out of all industrialized countries. Take a guess about how much the average American saves toward their retirement?

15%?	7%?	5%?
0%?	10%?	3%?
-2%?	3%?	21%?

Before I answer, let's see what people in other industrialized countries are saving. What countries are saving more. What countries are saving less. Check it out for yourself. The answers may surprise you.

	Savings Rate By Country		
Rank	Country	2010	2013
1	China	38.00%	50.00%
2	India	34.70%	32.00%
3	France	16.10%	15.80%
4	Germany	11.30%	13.60%
5	Turkey	19.50%	13.00%
6	Australia	8.90%	12.10%
7	Spain	13.90%	12.00%
8	Belgium	11.20%	10.60%
9	Switzerland	9.90%	9.50%
10	Portugal	10.20%	9.40%
11	Ireland	8.90%	9.10%
12	Sweden	8.50%	7.60%
13	United Kingdom	7.20%	7.50%
14	Austria	8.30%	7.30%
15	Poland	6.40%	7.00%
16	Brazil	7.00%	5.40%
17	Norway	6.10%	5.20%
18	Czech Republic	5.70%	4.90%
19	Italy	5.30%	4.50%
20	Canada	4.80%	4.30%
21	United States	5.30%	4.00%
22	Finland	4.10%	3.70%
23	Netherlands	3.90%	3.10%
24	Korea	4.30%	3.00%
25	Estonia	3.70%	1.90%
26	Japan	2.10%	1.60%
27	Hungary	2.50%	0.60%
28	New Zealand	0.10%	0.50%
29	Denmark	-0.20%	-1.80%

Well, the savings number is so small for most Americans, you might have missed the number: The answer is less than 5%. Our spending and savings looks like this:

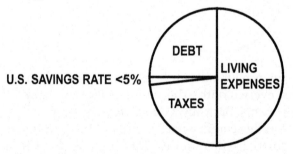

And get this: During the recession that started in 2008, the savings rate in America was in the negative! As a country of individuals, we borrowed more than we saved.

Today, those of us who are doing something towards our future are eking out a small sliver of savings. And even then, we may not be putting it in the right place with the right allocation. And it's all because we were never taught properly about how money works, and how we can get money to work hard for us.

Here's the problem in America: Most financial services are telling you that if you want to make the savings pie bigger, you need to prepare a budget and cut out some expenses. Stop eating out, stop going to Starbucks and stop putting your kids in summer camp.

But even if most people say they are willing to do it, it's just like being on a diet. The self-sacrifice only lasts for a short period of time, and then we are right back to our old habits.

So, we are going to do things differently. Instead, you are going to learn how to reduce your debt and legally cut your taxes, so we can free up this money and put it towards your savings.

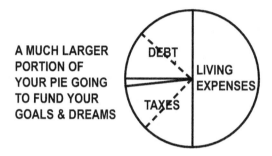

A MUCH LARGER PORTION OF YOUR PIE GOING TO FUND YOUR GOALS & DREAMS

Maybe you need some investments for the future to fund your retirement. Maybe you need a college fund for your children. Or an insurance program because you need to protect your assets and your family. Perhaps you want to leave a legacy to your family.

But here is the great thing, after you get going with a program, we're not taking any more money out of your pocket to accomplish these things. We're taking money you would ordinarily be paying to Uncle Sam and the bill collectors, and using those same dollars to do better things for you and your family.

So if we can do this, really cut people's debt and taxes, and then use this money help them build for their retirement, fund their children's education, and create wealth, tax-free, just like the rich ... Do you think many people would be interested to find out how?

Even though I can't hear it, I know the answer is, "Absolutely!"

And that brings me back to my Mission. I don't know how to reach everyone who wants to learn and do something about it. So I need your help in finding these people.

And that brings me to a problem: I don't have enough trainers that can help everyone that wants to learn. So I need your help in doing, or finding people that want to learn how to help others.

So, if you want to learn how to help yourself, read on!

And, if you want to learn how to help others, read on!

And, if you want to help me with my mission, read on!

SECTION II:

**HOW TO HARNESS YOUR PERSONAL POWER
& UNLOCK YOUR HIDDEN MOJO!**

"You are the embodiment of the information you choose
to accept and act upon. To change your circumstances
you need to change your thinking and subsequent actions."
— **Adlin Sinclair**

CHAPTER 11.
DIGGING FOR BURIED TREASURE: THE REAL
REASON WHY WE SHOULD DO WHAT WE DO.

About 95% of all Americans are broke at the end of the month: We don't have enough money to stop working, and we have to get back to work. Now about 5% of the people in this country do something different ...

But the unfortunate truth is that most of us do what we do, not because we love what we do, but because "It's a living." The next most unfortunate truth is that for most of us, it's not a very nourishing living ... financially, spiritually or Karmically. For a lot of us, we do what we do because "It pays the bills." Period.

Imagine getting up every morning at 7 a.m., running out the door to do your commute. Talking, listening, working – day after day, week after week, year after year after year. And what do you have to show for it? Year after year of paid bills, a couple of vacations per year, and the knowledge that you still have 25 years to go before you can collect Social Security. That is, if it's still around.

What you need to do is get focused on both your personal and your financial goals: Your reasons why you're doing what you're doing. What you want to obtain in the short, medium and long run. Sounds simple? It's not. Most of us are suffering from twin depressions: We are "Dream Dead" plus we have little or no clue on how to achieve what we think we want financially in life.

During the course of running internship programs, I've asked hundreds of college students why they go into their chosen profession. Most of the responses I get are tepid answers and platitudes: "I think I can get a good job when I graduate." "I can earn good money." "I want to help people, so I chose this field."

None of the answers really address the student's deep down "why."

Why do you want this job? Why do you want the money? What does the money represent for you? Why do you want to help people?

What I don't see often is a deep clear driving force that motivates and gives the person a passion to succeed.

My motivating desire to go to law school and become an attorney was to help other people. So that would be my external "why." But the deeper, underlying reason I wanted to help people was that when I was growing up I had a rough childhood at home and at school.

Then at 11 years old I had my first job working for a florist shop in New York City, running the cash register, doing floral arrangements and making deliveries. Next door was a fast food chicken place and Jim, the manager, would invite me over and treat me to lunch every so often. We would pull out a couple of crates, and we'd sit there holding our Styrofoam lunch trays and talk and eat. Here I was, a no-nothing 11 year old, and other successful adults were treating me with respect and really listening to what I had to say.

In high school, even though I was a C+ student at first, I noticed that many of the best teachers in the schools took a genuine interest in me, and what I thought. I knew that I couldn't ever repay the people that helped me deal with some difficult experiences growing up. But their actions towards me only served to reinforce my core belief that I needed to help other people during my lifetime.

So my "why" for becoming a lawyer was to repay past kindness and make a positive difference in people's lives.

And if you don't think that's enough of a motivating factor, it's exactly why you're able to benefit from this book. You see, after I did my legal internship with the Office of the Attorney General in Albany, New York, I was offered a position when I graduated. But what the job did for me was reinforce my belief that the profession wasn't about helping people – it was all about power and money. And that didn't fit into my "why." so I turned down the offer, and later quit law school.

That's WHY you're able to read this book. And now it's time for you to get real about your "Whys." You need to identify and understand the motivating factors in your life, and work hard toward achieving them.

Read on!

"The reason most people never reach their goals is that they don't define them, or ever seriously consider them as believable or achievable. Winners can tell you where they are going, what they plan to do along the way, and who will be sharing the adventure with them."
— **Denis Watley**

CHAPTER 12.
UNLOCKING YOUR DREAMS. ESTABLISHING YOUR GOALS.

Here's where you really get down to it. Your "Why" of "Whys" – So be as detailed as you can with your answers. But to dig this far down we have to go deep.

We're not going to be content with just scratching the surface and having you come up with platitudes: "Oh, I want to have a million in the bank by the time I retire."

ON-LINE WORKBOOK #2:
UNLOCKING YOUR DREAMS.

Time to go on-line and complete your workbook. What is it that you really want more of in your life? What's really missing? If you were to say one thing you that could have more of, what would that be?
  [ ] Time?   [ ] Money?   [ ] Travel?   [ ] Helping People?

What type of work do you do?
- What is your title?
- How long have you been doing it?
- How much do you earn annually?
- When was the last raise you received and how much was it for?
- How much is the top salary you think you can earn in your company?
- Share three things you love about your work.
- Share some things that are important to you about what you do.
- Share some things that you hate about your work.

Next ask yourself:
- Are you achieving your potential?
- Are you getting paid what you're worth?

- What do you think you're worth annually?
- How old are you now?
- How much do you have saved for your retirement?
- What age are you planning to retire?
- Geographically speaking, where would you like to retire?
- How much cash do you think you will need at retirement?
- Are you on target for reaching your retirement goals?
- How much are you short?
- Did you remember to adjust for taxation?

Where are you currently saving/investing for your retirement?
- Do you sometimes feel that you are gambling with your retirement by putting your money into the stock market?
- Would it be more comfortable if you got some guarantees such as never losing money & tax free income?
- Have you started saving for your son/daughter to go to college?
- Where are you saving now?

What is the most important thing in your life?
- Do you have Protection on the most important thing in your life?
- If money was no longer a concern to you, what would you be doing right now?
- Would you change your career?
- Have you ever thought about owning your own business?
- What are some of the reasons you want to be a business owner?
- Have you ever passed up something that you wished you hadn't?
- Why did you pass on it?

What are your goals now?
- Buy a new Home?
- Pay Off Your Mortgage?
- Buy a Luxury Car or Boat?
- Get More Free Time?
- Fully Fund Your Children's Education?
- Have Your Own Business?
- Take More Travel?
- Give Back & Helping Others?

Share three financial goals you have, and be specific.
1. Short term (6 months to 2 years):
2. Medium term (5-10 years):
3. Long term (20-40 years)

If you continue on the financial path that you're on now, on a scale of 1 to 5, how likely are you going to be able to achieve these goals?

$$1 = \text{Never} \quad 5 = 100\%$$

Whatever your answer, the time to start your "Personal Financial Plan" is now. The title of this book is **Act & Grow Rich!** Not "Think & Grow Rich." Not "Procrastinate & Grow Rich." Not "Contemplate & Grow Rich." But Act.

It's time to take control over your life, over your finances and over your future: You can have the life you want now and during your retirement. But the clock is ticking! Every day, week, month, year you wait, the more expensive and difficult it is to accomplish your goals. Agree? Good.

Now that you're fired up, slow down. To do something about it, you first have to understand where you are, and where you want to go. That's your Goals & Dreams, and we're working on that part.

Next you have to learn the Concepts behind "How Money Works." And that's what's up next. It's time to learn what they should have taught you in High School, College, Grad School, but didn't because companies, banks and Wall Street make money from you not knowing.

Time to "Know Up!"

Read on!

"When we are motivated by goals that have deep meaning, by dreams that need completion, by pure love that needs expressing, then we truly live life."
— **Greg Anderson**

CHAPTER 13:
UNDERSTANDING THE TWO BIGGEST "WHYS" IN YOUR LIFE: FAMILY & FREEDOM.

Whether we realize it or not our lives are full of cycles. Some are more obvious than others: We wake up every day, eat, excrete, work, eat, excrete, sleep, and then do it all over again the next day. Pretty basic cycle.

Then there are more complex cycles that cover longer periods of our lives. As children, our families are the center of our world. We then move into adolescence and young adulthood, and we become more self-centered and "Me" focused. We then cycle back to more of a family focus as we marry and have children of our own. And then during our retirement years our emphasis shifts back to "Me."

Since this isn't a psychology or sociology book, let's just take a quick look at each of the phases in the cycle, and see how it ties in to our "Why."

Now, I know some of you are muttering to yourselves, "Hey, I got this book to learn about making money and stuff. If I wanted "New Age" touchy feely stuff, I'd track down Oprah."

Yeah, yeah, yeah. Well this is about making money and stuff. So pipe down, and quit making assumptions, and you might just learn something helpful.

When we are children our family is our foundation. We are supported and loved, and form strong bonds to each other.

As we move through adolescence and into early adulthood, we become more "me" focused. We leave our families behind as our education and our work become more and more important.

Now, ask this person "Why are you getting an education? Why are you working?" And what are the answers? "To get a job." "So I can support myself."

Fast forward to when that person is married and ask the question, "Why are you working?" "So I can support my family." And so this part of the cycle continues for the next 20 or 30 years or so, only to be replaced by the last "Me" phase – the retirement years.

What is all boils down to is this: The reasons why we work so long and so hard are to provide for our family just as our family provided for us when we were growing up. Once we have done that, now it's to provide for ourselves in our retirement.

In short, it comes down to two words: Family. & Freedom.

We work hard in the hopes of providing more for our own family than our parents did for us. A bigger house. A debt free education for our children. More travel time.

And if we are part of the fortunate few, maybe we have enough to give back to our own parents to help provide for their retirement.

Think about that! Imagine having the financial means to pay for your parent's once in a lifetime $20,000 cruise vacation, or pay off their $135,000 mortgage, or buy them a $280,000 retirement home. All without blinking an eye at the cost.

Now, imagine you have built up enough for your own retirement. What would that look like?

> Taking vacations for four weeks at time to ports all over the world?
> Having a house on the water that you can escape to whenever the urge overtakes you?
> Visiting your children and grandchildren and having the means to stay in an expensive hotel for a week or two, and not even think twice about the expense?
> Buying that expensive sports car you fell in love with when you were a teenager?
> Or maybe funding a mission to help educate children?
> Or provide medicine or nutritional funding for the needy?
> Or building an orphanage?
> Or may be all of these things?

The simple truth is ... you could do all of these things if your head and heart were sold out to the ideas ... You're 100% committed. All in.

Understand your cycles. Understand your motivators. Understand the choice is yours.

Read on!

"Debt is the slavery of the free."
— **Publilius Syrus**

CHAPTER 14.
TWO KEY THINGS YOU NEED TO DO TO RETIRE RICH:
NUMERO UNO: RETIRE YOUR DEBT.

Now you've got a better understanding of your "Whys," it's time to move on to your "Hows." Remember "The Big Zero"? How you need to reduce your debt, and cut your taxes (legally) to build for your goals?

First, let's look at eight or nine basic debt management strategies. And don't fret, you can log-in to your online account and complete this section in your workbook.

#1. Figure Out Where You Spend Your Money. To get your debt under control, you have to first figure out your spending patterns. For one month, write down and log every penny you spend including cash, credit card and bank transfer. And that includes every $1 dollar doughnut and $2 cup of coffee. This will allow us to track how much of your spending is fixed and how much is discretionary (and easier to divert if necessary).

#2. Curb The Extras. Add up all your expenses on the list and plug in your monthly net income. If your expenses are lower than your income, congratulations. You can use the extra money to properly build for your goals. If your expenses exceed your income, you need to cut back on your discretionary spending. Controlling your coffee and doughnut habit or even your shopping fetish for a few months may help out quite a bit depending on how you apply your savings.

#3. Make A Debt List. You can use the spreadsheet to tag your debt obligations, then add in interest you're charged on each. Next sort them by interest rate going from highest to lowest. (Don't worry about getting stuck on how to do the software stuff, we'll help you through this when you do your workbook section. Just worry about the numbers!)

#4. Get A New "0" Interest Card Or Low Interest Credit Card. Put all new charges on the card with the lowest interest rate and pay the minimum balance each month.

#5. Pay Off The Highest Interest Rate Card First. Look over your list and allocate the maximum you can afford to pay to the balance with the highest interest rate. Pay the minimum on all other revolving bills. Make sure you pay early on all your cards. One late payment can trigger a late fee and a huge jump in monthly interest charges.

#6. Move Down The List. Once you wipe out highest rate, put your money toward paying the debt with the next highest rate. If you have a credit card with a low introductory rate that will go up after a fixed amount of time, be sure to track the date it switches and reorganize your list. If the rate is significantly higher than your other debt, you may want to eliminate that balance before the low rate expires.

#7. Lower Your Fixed Expenses. Everyone should be constantly looking at steps they can do to lower their household bills. If you own your own home, see if it's cost effective to refinance your mortgage to get a lower interest rate. If you have a good credit score and payment history, ask your credit card company to lower your interest rate. Ask your cable TV provider for any specials deals that can lower your monthly charges. Find a better deal and ask them to match or threaten to leave. Do the same for your cell phone bill. (but don't leave if your still under contract. You don't want to get hit with an early termination fee.)

#8. Boost Your Income. Do you get a big tax refund every year? If you do, it means too much is being withheld from your paycheck. Reduce your withholding by changing your W-4 at work and put the extra income towards your goals. You can also consider adding another income stream that you can use to pay off debt and build wealth. (More on this option later in the book.)

Optional #9. Transfer High-Interest Balances. You may have received a special offer from one of your credit card companies to transfer other debt to their card in order to reduce the interest rate you're paying on the balance. Be careful of the fine print. There may be high transfer fees assessed up front on the entire balance, even if the monthly rate is low. And the low rate may only be in effect for a limited time, and then jump considerably.

Remember, your credit score is affected by a high debt-to-available-credit ratio. So keep an eye out on your balances. Now, let's handle the bullies in the room, and deal with your debt.

Managing your debt is the first strategy.

The second thing you need to work on is reducing your taxes. Legally, of course. This is such an important aspect of how you become financially independent, we'll devote many sections in the book to this topic including a portion of the next chapter.

For now, let's handle the bullies in the room and deal with your debt!

ON-LINE WORKBOOK #3:
YOUR EXPENSE LIST SPREADSHEET:
ELIMINATE THE NEGATIVE.

How You Allocate Your Money			
DAILY LIVING	**DEBT**	**HEALTH**	**SAVINGS**
Groceries	Student Loan	Health Insurance	Emergency Fund
Personal Supplies	Other Loan	Doctor/Dentist	Transfer to Savings
Clothing	Credit Card Debt	Medicine/Drugs	Retirement (401k, IRA)
Cleaning	Alimony/Child Support	Health Club Dues	Investments
Education/Lessons		Life Insurance	Education
Dining/Eating Out	**TAXES**	Veterinarian/Pet Care	
Salon/Barber	Federal Taxes		**INCOME**
Pet Food	State/Local Taxes	**ENTERTAINMENT**	Wages & Tips
		Videos/DVDs	Interest Income
HOME EXPENSES	**MISCELLANEOUS**	Music	Dividends
Mortgage/Rent	Bank Fees	Games	Gifts Received
Home/Rental Insurance	Postage	Rentals	Refunds/Reimbursements
Electricity		Movies/Theater	Transfer From Savings
Gas/Oil	**TRANSPORTATION**	Concerts/Plays	
Water/Sewer/Trash	Vehicle Payments	Books	
Phone	Auto Insurance	Hobbies	
Cable/Satellite	Fuel	Film/Photos	
Internet	Bus/Taxi/Train Fare	Sports	
Furnishings/Appliances	Repairs	Outdoor Recreation	
Lawn/Garden	Registration/License	Toys/Gadgets	
Maintenance/Supplies		Vacation/Travel	
Improvements	**CHARITY/GIFTS**		
	Gifts Given	**SUBSCRIPTIONS**	
	Charitable Donations	Newspaper	
	Religious Donations	Magazines	
		Dues/Memberships	

SECTION III:
THE SECRET TO YOUR SUCCESS.

PART I:
ALBERT EINSTEIN.

"Being rich is having money; being wealthy is having time."
— **Margaret Bonnano**

CHAPTER 15.
THE FIVE FACTORS FOR BUILDING WEALTH.

First of all, if you walk down the street asking people the question, "Do you want to build wealth?" Everyone is going to say that they want to build wealth, isn't that true? Well then, if everyone wants to do, then how come the vast majority of us — like 99% of us — don't?

I mean, you're smart, right? I'm reasonably intelligent. Most of the people who graduate from college aren't idiots, right?

So, why is this so difficult for us to accomplish?

Think of it this way. If you wanted to drive from New York to Florida do you think it would be helpful to have a road map? Or, better still, a GPS?

Otherwise, what's going to happen? You going to get in your car and drive and hope that you're going South. Eventually you may get there, but going to take you a lot longer, and cost you a lot more money.

Building wealth is the same thing. So what does this really tell you? You need to have a plan and start early! And these are the issues that you have to consider to be successful at managing your money.

The Five Factors For Building Wealth:
Factor #1. Money.

First off, you don't need don't need to invest 5,000 dollars a month, so relax. There's a misconception that you need to put in a lot of money to build wealth. You just need to make the commitment to start and do it at whatever level you can regularly afford.

Factor #2. Time.

The money that you do put away on regular basis, you need to do it long-term. Month after month, year after year. You can't put it away for one year, five years or even 10 years. You need to put it away for 20 or 30 years ideally or as long as you possibly can. So the earlier you start the better.

Factor #3. Positive Rate of Return.

Thirdly, you have to get a positive, not a negative rate of return your money. We all know what a positive rate of return is, right? Stick our money in a 5-Year CD at the bank and earn 1% interest? That's considered positive.

What is a negative rate of return? When you buy one of the new 70" 4K Smart TVs for $2,500, and you put it on your credit card. Then when the bill comes in, you don't pay off the balance right away. That's a negative return because of the interest rate you're being charged. It's going cost you a tremendous amount more if you don't pay the negative high interest charges off.

Factor #4: Inflation.

When you get a return on your money, you have to outpace inflation. What is inflation? It's simply when the cost of goods in the future keep rising and your purchasing power doesn't keep pace, because income wages are not rising as fast.

Let's take an example. If you are going to buy an inexpensive new car today, how much will it cost? Let's say $20,000. 30 years ago, how much money does that car cost? A lot less, under $5,000. 30 years from now, what do you think that car is going to cost? How about around $80,000. That's inflation. And if your income doesn't rise commensurately, you going to lose money due to decreased buying power.

You can see the effects of inflation all around you in the cost of these basic items:

Effects of Inflation On Your Money			
Item	**Cost in 1950**	**Cost in 1985**	**Cost in 2015**
Postage Stamp	3¢ Stamp	22¢ Stamp	49¢ Stamp
Milk	82¢ Gallon	$1.98 Gallon	$4.50 Gallon
Eggs	60¢ Dozen	80¢ Dozen	$2.09 Dozen
Bread	14¢ Pound	74¢ Pound	$1.44 Pound
Gasoline	30¢ Gallon	$1.24 Gallon	$2.85 Gallon
College Education	$625 Year	$9,525 Year	$49,536 Year

(University of Pennsylvania)

Factor #5: Taxation.

As we discussed before, taxation is the single biggest reason that prevents people from becoming financially independent. If you are not doing something to lessen the burden of taxation, you're in for a tremendous uphill battle. Conjure up the image of yourself as a Sisyphus from Greek mythology and you get the idea.

Remember, what we said about the deficit? The government reports it as about $18,000,000,000,000. (You know differently now, don't you?) If you want to get an idea of how much a trillion dollars is, think about this:

If you had $30 million dollars a year to spend, do you know how long it would take you to spend it? I'll give you a hint. You're way off base. I was. Totally. The number is mind-blowing!

You would have to spend $30,000,000 a year for over 33,000 years! That's how much a trillion dollars is. It's a whole lot of money. And as a nation, we are literally $80,000,000,000 in debt and counting. Can you say "higher taxes"?

Now, do you see the importance of taking responsibility for your own finances and not leaving it up to the government, banks, Wall Street and companies?

If you want to know what to do about it ...

Read on!

"Our attitude toward life determines life's attitude towards us."
— **John N. Mitchell**

CHAPTER 16.
HOW TO MANAGE RESPONSIBILITY WHILE
BUILDING WEALTH: THE X-CURVE LIFESTYLE.

What does being financially independent mean to you? Having a million in the bank? Having a home with the mortgage paid off? Having enough money to travel twice a year?

This is what I use as my definition: "Financial independence is the ability to live the lifestyle you wish, off of the interest that your assets generate, without having to spend down your principle."

Have you ever heard of the X-Curve before? I'm guessing that even if studied finance, economics or business, the answer would be "No." I was an English major, went to law school, and am a business owner. So you can bet that before I went through my practical financial education, I'd never heard of it either!

The X-Curve is a simple but very powerful concept that you should understand and follow to better achieve your objectives. The main premise is that everybody goes through two cycles in their life: When you are younger and when you older. So right now, you are still younger so you have a lot of responsibilities to take care of.

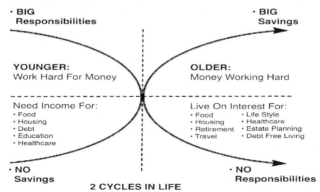

You have the basics like food and clothing. But you may have a lot more as well. Do you have children? Do you rent or own a house? You have mortgage? Do you take care of your parents? Do you have loans or other types of debt?

So what pays for your responsibilities? Your job. And after you pay all of the responsibilities, you probably don't have that much money left over. I am not sure what you save, but if it's like most Americans it's not much. Almost all of your money is already gone toward this many responsibilities.

Well, the money you have left over, if you put in the right place, that money will continue to build wealth for you.

And as you get older, you want your responsibilities to be a lot less. Your children have finished college, you've finished paying for your house, and you're managing your debt.

But you still have some responsibilities, yes? Food, clothing, taxes. So, the question now is, "You want to enjoy your retirement?" What would you like to do when you retire? Whatever it is, chances are you will need money to do that, right? Or do you want to stay home most of the time sitting on the couch watching TV and eating dinners from the microwave?

Probably not the way you envisioned your retirement when you were working, yes?

And you also have to take care of your health. As you get older, what can happen to your health? It deteriorates, it gets worse. And that can be a major blow to your finances.

So, what pays for your responsibilities is how strong you build your wealth. Because as you get older, your money has to take care of these responsibilities. While you are younger, you can work to pay for these responsibilities. When you are older, even if you want to work, no company might want to hire you for a decent paying job.

And what two companies are the largest employers of people over 60 in America? Walmart and McDonalds. These people didn't properly plan for their retirement. They lived too long, and they ran out of money so they couldn't stop working and enjoy life.

So these are two problems you have. First, when you are younger, you need to take care of your responsibilities, God forbid, anything should happen. You need to have a game plan for these responsibilities because you don't have a lot of money to take care of them on your own.

Second, when you get older, you want to keep as much as that money for yourself. So you want to minimize your taxation from Uncle Sam. And in a little bit I'm going to share with you what that solution is.

But first, how do you take care of your responsibilities? One very effective way is by utilizing risk management. And, how you manage your risk is by transferring these responsibilities to an insurance company.

Let me ask you, **What's Your Greatest Asset?** And if it's your greatest asset, shouldn't you have protection on it?

If you own a car you have insurance. If you own house you have insurance. A lot people even have insurance on their cell phones. If you had an ATM machine in your home that spit out $3,000, $5,000, $10,000 a month, month after month after month, wouldn't you insure it?

Of course you would.

Well, you are that ATM for your family! You are your greatest asset! Each month you bring in your income to the household and it goes right out the door again in the form of living expenses, debt and taxes. Remember "The Big Zero?"

Now, what if something unexpected happened to you, and it was lights out? Game over. Curtains. Planting daisy time?

What would happen to your family? Would they be able to still afford the house? Would your children still be able to attend the school of their choice?

Or would your spouse have to get another job? Sell the house? Put your children to work? Postpone their education?

So, when you're younger, the issue you have to address is what we call "Living Too short." And the solution to this problem is through proper insurance and risk management.

When you are older, the second issue have to address is called "Living Too Long." It's the real possibility of outliving your money, and suffering because of it.

In a Harris Interactive survey, 66% of the adults surveyed between the ages of 45 and 65 were more afraid of living too long, than dying too early!

It almost goes without saying, but I'll say it anyway: "Quality of Life" really matters. And understanding and following the X-Curve lifestyle is how your reach your goals.

But you know what the problem is here in the U.S.? Very few people live in an X-curve lifestyle. Most people live in a straight line: Paycheck to paycheck. Yet many people still believe that their Uncle Sam is going take care of them with Social Security.

Did you know that when the government started Social Security there were 45 people working and paying into the fund for every one person collecting benefits?

And do you what the ratio is today? It's down to 2.8 people paying in to every one person getting benefits. That's shocking. The Social

Security system is going to be broke in 2033 according to the governments own projections.

If, by some miracle, it's still around by the time you retire, the government will have pushed back the age you need to be to get the benefits until you're in your late 70s or maybe early 80s.

On top of that they will probably have to freeze or cut the dollar amount of the benefits as well just to keep the system afloat.

So you know the social security statement that you get in the mail that says you're going to get $2,000 dollars a month in the future? Imagine that amount never changes. The same dollar amount, maybe 30 years from now, that $2,000 dollars. So when you go out you have a nice dinner, go see a movie; well, that's pretty much what your benefits check pays for.

If I were you, I wouldn't plan on it being a tremendous help for your retirement.

So, what's the solution to these twin issues of **Living Too Short** and **Living Too Long?** Simply, where you put your money.

Putting your money in the right place, with the right allocation, and following "The Five Factors For Building Wealth" is the key.

X-CURVE
RULE OF RESPONSIBILTY & WEALTH

"The most powerful force in the universe is compound interest."
— **Albert Einstein**

CHAPTER 17.
UNLOCKING THE "8TH WONDER OF THE WORLD."

You work so hard for your money, don't you? But have you ever thought about how money works? One of the main ways is through "The Rule of 72."

Have you heard of "The Rule of 72?" Well, like most of the financial concepts in this book, unfortunately it wasn't something I had heard of either. But it was formulated by a rather smart guy named Albert Einstein. Him I've heard of!

The rule states that if you know the rate of return and divide it into the number 72, it will show you how many years it will take for your money to double.

Something along these lines:

$$\frac{72}{RR} = YR\$^2$$

Now, let me ask you, "What do you do with whatever money you have left at the end of the month? Assuming you don't spend it, that is."

If you're like most people, you put into the bank where you earn a little over "Zero" interest. And if you put your money in a CD (Certificate of Deposit), the bank would pay you a whopping 1% return!

So 1% goes into 72 how many times? 72. That's how many years will take for your money to double. 72.

I don't know about you, but I don't have too many cycles of 72 in my bones to wait around. But let's say you put $10,000 away today, 72 years later your Grandkids will see it double.

Is it any wonder that the banks don't want you to know about this? Imagine if the banks were required to put this information on their posters!

"Highest interest on a 5-year CD! 1%! See your money double in the year 2190."

No one would be putting their money in bank!

Now, let's say I have somewhere you can put your money and get a 4% return. Would want to put your money there? Compared to 1%? Heck yes! So let's look at how this works: 72 divided by 4, is 18. So every 18 years your money doubles.

Let's pretend you are 29 years old right now, and you have $10,000 to invest. Here's what will happen with your money:

72/4% RR = 18 Years

29	$10,000
47	$20,000
65	$40,000

Not bad, a heck of lot better than 1%. But can you retire on $40,000? Don't think so. But do you know what another major problem is?

Inflation.

Over the past 10-20 years inflations is running at about 3%-4% per year. So here's the problem: $10,000 today may buy you a used car, but I guarantee you that 30 years from now you will need $40,000 to buy the same type of used car.

So if you get a 4% return on your money you're basically guaranteeing that you'll be broke further down the road.

But most people think, "4% is great!" But wealthy people, money people, aren't most people. Wealthy people know not to settle for 4 percent.

You know what rich people do? They seek out another investment and get a better return. Imagine you could get a 12% return. 72 divided by 12? Your money would double every six years. How's that going to look? Instead of $40,000 maybe you'll have three times as much, $120,000? Let's see.

72/12% RR = 6 Years

29	$10,000
35	$20,000
41	$40,000
47	$80,000
53	$160,000
59	$360,000
65	$640,000

It's the same time period. The only thing that changed was the rate of return you got on your money!

So, instead of getting three times your money when you triple the interest rate, the extra interest is earning you more and more money. And that's the beauty of compounding!

		Annual Compounding Table			
		4% Rate of Return		**12% Rate of Return**	
Year	Age	Principal	Interest	Principal	Interest
1	29	$10,000	$400	$10,000	$1,200
2	30	$10,400	$416	$11,200	$1,344
3	31	$10,816	$433	$12,544	$1,505
4	32	$11,249	$450	$14,049	$1,686
5	33	$11,699	$468	$15,735	$1,888
6	34	$12,167	$487	$17,623	$2,115
7	35	$12,653	$506	$19,738	$2,369
8	36	$13,159	$526	$22,107	$2,653
9	37	$13,686	$547	$24,760	$2,971
10	38	$14,233	$569	$27,731	$3,328
11	39	$14,802	$592	$31,058	$3,727
12	40	$15,395	$616	$34,785	$4,174
13	41	$16,010	$640	$38,960	$4,675
14	42	$16,651	$666	$43,635	$5,236
15	43	$17,317	$693	$48,871	$5,865
16	44	$18,009	$720	$54,736	$6,568
17	45	$18,730	$749	$61,304	$7,356
18	46	$19,479	$779	$68,660	$8,239
19	47	$20,258	$810	$76,900	$9,228
20	48	$21,068	$843	$86,128	$10,335
21	49	$21,911	$876	$96,463	$11,576
22	50	$22,788	$912	$108,038	$12,965
23	51	$23,699	$948	$121,003	$14,520
24	52	$24,647	$986	$135,523	$16,263
25	53	$25,633	$1,025	$151,786	$18,214
26	54	$26,658	$1,066	$170,001	$20,400
27	55	$27,725	$1,109	$190,401	$22,848
28	56	$28,834	$1,153	$213,249	$25,590
29	57	$29,987	$1,199	$238,839	$28,661
30	58	$31,187	$1,247	$267,499	$32,100
31	59	$32,434	$1,297	$299,599	$35,952
32	60	$33,731	$1,349	$335,551	$40,266
33	61	$35,081	$1,403	$375,817	$45,098
34	62	$36,484	$1,459	$420,915	$50,510
35	63	$37,943	$1,518	$471,425	$56,571
36	64	$39,461	$1,578	$527,996	$63,360
37	65	**$41,039**	**$1,642**	**$591,356**	**$70,963**

This is the power of compounding. Is it any wonder that Albert Einstein called it the "8th Wonder of the World?" Powerful stuff, yes?

Well, wait until you see what's coming next!

Read on!

"Taxation is just a sophisticated way of
demanding money with menaces."
— **Terry Pratchett**

CHAPTER 18.
TAX NOW. TAX LATER. TAX NEVER?
NEVER HEARD OF IT!

Now, let me share with you the places where most people put their money. The first place is called "Tax Now."

TAX NOW is when you put your money in the bank and earn interest. Whether you make $10 or $10,000 in interest, you have to pay taxes on it. So, you put money in a savings account? You have a CD? You have stocks? Then you have to pay taxes every single year.

For illustration purposes, let's say you're earning 12%, and your money is in a **Tax Now** account. You're paying taxes year after year on your earnings. If your tax rate is at 35%, taxes are knocking your earnings down to 8% per year.

Applying the **Rule of 72** to an 8% rate of return, your money will double every nine years. But as the table below shows, **when you go from 12% down to 8% you're losing almost $500,000 to taxes!**

The Rule Of 72								
4% Money Doubles:		**8% Money Doubles:**		**12% Money Doubles:**	
(72 / 4%) = 18 Years		**(72 / 8%) = 9 Years**		**(72 / 12%) = 6 Years**	
Age	4%	Age	8%	Age	12%
29	$ 10,000	29	$ 10,000	29	$ 10,000
47	$ 20,000	38	$ 20,000	35	$ 20,000
65	**$ 40,000**	47	$ 40,000	41	$ 40,000
		56	$ 80,000	47	$ 80,000
		65	**$ 160,000**	53	$ 160,000
				39	$ 320,000
				65	**$ 640,000**

That's the effect that taxes has on our money!

TAX LATER. Some people say, "I have a 401(k) retirement plan. I have an IRA. My taxes are deferred." And that is correct. It also means that Uncle Sam is investing along with you and sharing in your future profits. Big time.

Let's say at age 29 you put $10,000 of your earnings into a 401(k) plan, and you saved 35% ($3,500) in taxes that year. At age 65 your $10,000 grew to $640,000.

You're happy that your money grew because you need it for your retirement, yes? But then, when you pull it out, you discover that your tax rate is now at 40%, 45%, 50%, 60%. Year after year after year!

So let me ask you, "Would you be happy because you saved a few thousand in taxes while you were working and could afford to pay it?" Or when you discovered it would cost 50 or even 100 times as much in lost income, would you want "… to throttle the person at your company that advised you to take the match and be happy?"

See, once upon a time you saved $3,500 in taxes. Now, you have to pay $300,000 in taxes. This is what is in store for you when you have Uncle Sam investing along with you.

Still think 401(k) plans are such a great deal? No? But this is what most people do because they don't know of any alternative.

Well, let me show you there is a third way. It's called tax advantage or "Tax Never" and most people, probably 95% of the population, don't even know it exists.

TAX NEVER. You already know that wealthy people control Washington. They control politics. And they control the tax code. They created this code so they don't need to pay taxes on the money they make. It's as simple as that.

Can you think of any place where you can put your money and not have to pay taxes? I'll wait.

Ok, you know about a Roth IRA? It's an Individual Retirement Account where a person can put up to $5,500 a year, and take it out tax-free. But there are restrictions and penalties if you earn too much or want to take it out before you reach 59 and a half years old.

The rich don't put money into Roth IRAs. They make way too much money to qualify, and it wouldn't give them the compounding they want from larger amounts.

The rich put their money into plans where they can grow their money, risk-free and tax-free.

Ever heard of Internal Revenue Code 7702? Nope? Well, I hadn't either. Wall Street trained financial advisors only push products they are licensed to sell. And they sell only products they earn commissions on. And those products generally fall into "Tax Now" and "Tax Later" accounts. Each group relies on a different strategy to earn its rate of return.

Taxation & Your Money		
1	**2**	**3**
TAX NOW	**TAX LATER**	**TAX NEVER**
Checking	401(k) / 403(b) / 457	Roth IRA
Savings	IRA / SEP / SIMPLE	College Fund
CDs	Pension Plan	MUNIs
Stocks	Annuities	IRC 7702
Mutual Funds	TSP (Thrift Savings)	
	457 (Government)	

Tax Now accounts are **Fixed** accounts and they earn very low returns.

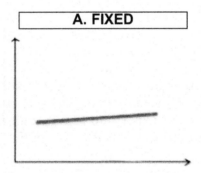

A. FIXED

Tax Deferred or **Tax Later** accounts are **Variable**, they go up and down according to the market. The returns can be much higher, but there is also much greater risk as well.

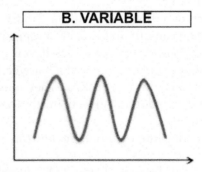

B. VARIABLE

Tax Advantage or **Tax Never** accounts. Surprise! Surprise! Surprise! Rich people have a third place they put their money in. It's called an

"Index." An **Index** strategy combines the best qualities of **Fixed** and **Variable** together.

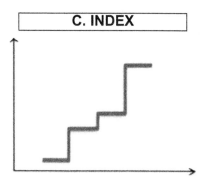

Index accounts have guarantees. There is a floor. And there is a ceiling. So your money can only go in one direction: And that's UP.

When the market goes up. You get the gains up to the ceiling or cap. When the market loses, your money is 100% protected by the floor. Whether the market drops 10%, 20%, 30% or 50% – **YOU NEVER LOSE MONEY!**

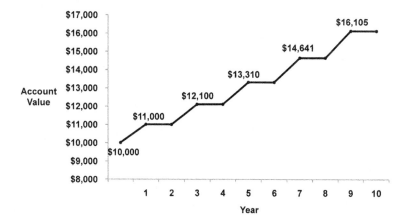

So if you had a choice today about where to earn your money, what would you choose? Would you be more interested in safety? Risk with the possibility of greater rewards? Or indexed where your money has only one direction to go? Up.

ACTION ALERT #7:
TIME TO PLAY THE MATCH GAME.

AND IF YOU WANT AN INDEX FROM A 7702 PLAN? YOU ALSO GET TAX NEVER.

So what do you have now? Where are you investing or saving now? Look at the charts. You have B and 2? You have A and 1? But the most important question is: "Do you have C and 3?"

Maybe now that you know a little more, you might want to diversify your investments. You don't want to put all your eggs in one basket. Well, I'm going to share with you how you can take advantage of an Index to do just that.

Indexes follow Internal Revenue Code just like 401(k) plans. They have a number too. It's under IRC Tax Code 7702, and it governs life insurance and taxation.

Remember who controls Washington? Rich lawyers who are politicians who write the Tax Code. And who benefits from the code most? The poor? The Middle Class? Or the Rich?

Nuff said.

Read on!

"The process by which banks create money
is so simple that the mind is repelled."
— **John Kenneth Galbraith**

CHAPTER 19.
WHY BANKS FAIL 95% OF US (AND LOVE IT)

Where do most people put their money after they get paid? In the bank. And why do you put in the bank? Because it's safe and you can earn some money back.

The reason why it's safe is because of the FDIC, that's the Federal Depository Insurance Corporation. And you know how much you're insured for? Up to $250,000. Now most people I know don't have $250,000 in their account, but they feel better knowing that whatever they have is insured.

Another reason why people put their money in the bank is because they are going to earn some money back. Some interest. But the banks are paying basically 0%. And when you tie your money up long-term in a 3-year, 5-year CD, you can earn up to 1%

Now, the banks work on something called a "1 to 3" rule. They take in your money, my money, everyone's money, and for every $1 they take in they're able to lend out $3.

When the banks got into trouble in 2008, it was because they lent out too much money and over extended themselves. Over 300 banks went belly up and were taken over by the government.

So the banks take our money, and then they like to lend it back to us. Do you have credit cards? If you do you might be paying 18 to 29 percent interest. You know that the highest interest rate banks charge for credit cards is over 60%! Before Congress deregulated the banking industry anything over 18% was considered usury. Basically loan sharking. Charging high interest rates was what the Mafia did before they broke your kneecaps, if you didn't pay them back in a timely manner. And our politicians have allowed the banking industry to legally act like the mob when it comes to money.

If you have a car loan you could be paying 7 to 12 percent interest. If you have a mortgage, 4 to 6%, and of course the banks charge all types of fees and penalties on top of that too.

We know the banks like to make as much money as possible. But there is another place where they put their money in order to get better protection and higher rates of return.

The banks put their money into insurance companies. The insurance companies insure client accounts through the SIPC. The Securities Investor Protection Corporation. Each account is insured up to $500,000 and insurance companies pull together billions and billions and billions upon billions of dollars every month. They are able to pay out higher rates of return from 8 to 15 percent, than we can normally get.

Insurance companies work on a "3 to 1" rule. For every 3 dollars they take in they are only able to lend out 1 dollar. So actually they are six times safer than the banks.

Now, where do you think the rich put their money? In the bank earning 0% interest? Or in insurance companies where they can get a much better return?

And this is what we do for our clients. We cut out the bank or the middleman and we put our clients directly into insurance companies where they can get asset protection and a much better rate of return just like the rich.

Look at the top right side of the graph. This is what the top 5% of the population does. The rich put their money into insurance companies. And here is what the middle class and poorer people do, they put their money into the bank where it earns basically nothing.

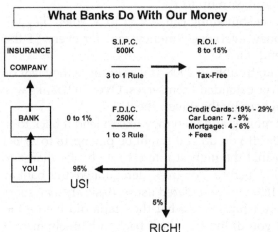

Which side would you like to be on? The rich of course.

Now, I'm going to show you how you can take advantage of the same programs as the wealthy. So hang on to your seat belt. It's going to be a wild ride.

Read on!

"Everything the working class has been told to do,
the rich do not do. That is my message."
— Robert Kiyosaki

CHAPTER 20.
THE CLASH OF THE TITANS: THE ROTH IRA VS. THE IUL

I want to show you an example of what we do for people. Let's turn back the clock. the date is now 1998, and you have $100,000 that you put into a Roth mutual fund. At the end of 1998, the market rose over 28%. You'd be happy, right? Next year the market rose 21%, and you'd still be very happy.

But the market goes up. The market goes down. The market goes up. The market goes down. At the end of 2012, your average return was 6.3 percent. Your money went from $100,000 in 1998 to over $292,000 in 2012. It almost doubled during that time-frame. Overall, you'd be happy, yes? Okay.

Roth Mutual Fund / IRA		
		$ 100,000.00
1998	28.60%	$ 128,580.00
1999	21.00%	$ 155,633.23
2000	-9.10%	$ 141,470.61
2001	-11.90%	$ 124,649.75
2002	-22.10%	$ 97,102.16
2003	28.70%	$ 124,951.06
2004	10.90%	$ 138,545.73
2005	4.90%	$ 145,348.33
2006	15.80%	$ 168,298.83
2007	5.50%	$ 177,538.43
2008	-37.00%	$ 111,849.21
2009	26.50%	$ 141,444.51
2010	15.10%	$ 162,731.91
2011	2.10%	$ 166,165.56
2012	16.00%	$ 192,752.05
	6.30%	

Now, let's say instead you put your $100,000 into an IUL account. As you know, IUL's have caps or ceilings on earnings. In this particular account the cap is 13%. So in 1998, instead of earning 28%, you earn up to the 13% ceiling. The next year, instead of earning 21% you earned the cap of 13%.

The market goes up. The market goes down. But when the market goes down, here you have a guaranteed floor. So when the market losses money, it doesn't matter how much it losses, you are insulated. Your money is 100% safe.

At the end of that same time period, your return averaged 7.6%. It's only 1.3% more than the Roth IRA account. That's not a big difference in terms of percentages, but look at the difference in how much cash you accumulated.

You went from a $100,000 in 1998 to over $295,000 in 2012. That's over $100,000 more than someone who had their money invested in the market. Their money was subject to market loss. Your money isn't.

IUL Cash Value / 7702 Policy		
		$100,000.00
1998	13.00%	$113,000.00
1999	13.00%	$127,690.00
2000	.00%	$127,690.00
2001	.00%	$127,690.00
2002	.00%	$127,690.00
2003	13.00%	$144,289.70
2004	11.00%	$160,161.57
2005	5.00%	$168,169.65
2006	13.00%	$190,031.70
2007	5.50%	$200,483.44
2008	.00%	$200,483.44
2009	13.00%	$226,546.29
2010	13.00%	$255,997.31
2011	2.10%	$261,373.25
2012	13.00%	$295,351.77
	7.64%	

That is because when you get your earnings within an IUL, your gains are locked in annually. Your gains become principle, and you always earn on your gains.

Warren Buffet said there are basic two principles to build financial independence. The first principle is "Never lose money." The second principle is, "to always follow the first principle." And that is the advantage that you get.

Now, on top of that if your money had been in the stock market, mutual funds or 401(k) plans, these are all subject to taxation. So, let's say you needed to take that money out, the $192,000. Do you think your taxes are going to be higher or lower in the future? My bet is they're going to be higher.

We already talked about that before in terms of the deficit. It's literally $80 trillion dollars not the $18 trillion the government tells us. In addition to that, we've also have the expenses associated with climate change, crumbling infrastructure and the high cost of medicine. All these things need to be paid for, and guess who's going to pay for it? Yep, you are. Well, to be fair, not all of it. Just a high percentage per capita. But you get the point.

So, when you need the money the most for your retirement or for health reasons, you might be subject to 40%, 45% even 50% in taxes. Instead of you getting the full $192,000, you're going to write a whopper of a check to the government. That's the effect of taxation on your money.

Now, I don't know about you, but I'm not too happy about that. When I need that money most, I want to be able to use all of it – not give away half of it to Uncle Sam. I'm all in favor us paying our fair share of taxes, but we also have the right to try to legally minimize our taxes, just like the rich do for themselves and thier family.

Stocks, Mutual Funds & 401K Plans Are All Subject To Taxes:

$192,752 × 35% Tax Rate = You Pay an Additional $67,463 to Uncle Sam
$192,752 × 40% Tax Rate = You Pay an Additional $77,100 to Uncle Sam
$192,752 × 45% Tax Rate = You Pay an Additional $86,738 to Uncle Sam
$192,752 × 50% Tax Rate = You Pay an Additional $96,376 to Uncle Sam

What Account Would You Rather Have When You Retire?

401(k)?   IUL?

Not 'Nuff said.
Read on!

"Everything you want is out there waiting for you to ask. Everything you want also wants you. But you have to take action to get it."
— Jules Renard

CHAPTER 21.
THE SWISS ARMY KNIFE OF FINANCIAL SERVICES.

Think about some of the financial programs out there designed to help you achieve your goals: CDs, Mutual Funds, IRAs, 401(k)s, stocks. Many of these vehicles are one-trick ponies. They offer one positive benefit in the "Plus" or "Pros" column, and usually several negatives in the "Cons" column.

THERE ARE 17 DIFFERENT BENEFITS
TO MOST 7702/IUL PLANS!

1. Death Benefit: In an IUL plan you pay a small amount of money to secure and ensure a large amount of protection for your family, and yourself.

Let's say you put aside $500 a month, $6,000 per year, into your bank account. At the end of three years, your account would have increased to $18,000. If something, God forbid, happened to you, you're family would only get the $18,000 to use for your funeral expenses (providing it wasn't tied up in probate) because you're not going to make much on the interest, and you're losing money through inflation.

On the other hand if you put that money in the stock market you most assuredly would have $18,000 three years down the road. You might have 24,000. You might have $9,000. You just don't know.

Regardless, neither of these options is going to give your family any sort of return that is going to make a difference in their lives for any appreciable length of time.

Depending on your premium, your IUL policy may pay out to your family a Death Benefit of $1,000,000. Unlike car, home, phone, and other insurance policies that people take out, pay into year after year, and never use. One day you will certainly pass from this mortal coil (i.e., die), and when that happens you have a 100% guaranteed payout to your beneficiaries. That's called proper risk management.

2. Cash Accumulation: Depending on how you set-up and pay into your account, you have the potential for cash accumulation with penalty-free and tax-free access at any point of time. It represents a return of the after-tax money.

3. Protection Against Market Loss: IUL accounts have what is called a "Guaranteed Floor" that protects you against ever having a negative return due to market losses.

4. The Annual Reset Provision: At the end of each 12-month period you capture and lock in each positive return in the market. The annual growth in the policy's cash value gets locked in to the principal, and is the policyholders to keep forever.

Contrast this with the stock market where the gains are only paper gains until they are withdrawn. But because your gains are not locked in with a guaranteed floor, you can have paper gains for five years in row, and then lose everything and more, when the stock market craters.

5. Upside Growth Potential: When the market or index rises, your account participates in the growth up to the ceiling or cap on your particular account. The growth for some IULs have approached 10% annually over the past 25 years.

6. Tax-Deferred Growth: This is another essential element in an IUL account: Cash values grow tax-deferred, and they become tax-free under certain conditions (see #7). It's important not to cancel or withdraw more than the limits to prevent income tax.

7. Tax-free Access to Cash Accumulation: Whether you take out a loan to buy a car or a house, the loans are tax-free. The same principle holds true for life insurance. You can borrow back your cash value tax-free. This is called the Policy Loan Provision.

8. No Minimum Age Or Income Requirement: Unlike IRA or SEP plans where a minimum age and income is required in order to contribute, IULs can be set up for any age, including infants. This can add 20 years of tax-deferred growth to your account resulting in a tremendous increase in cash accumulation in later years.

9. No Mandatory Distribution: In general, IRA and 401(k) plans force you to begin liquidating accounts at a mandatory age. IULs avoid that burden as well as other bureaucratic red tape of traditional tax-qualified plans.

10. Access At Any Age: In general, people retire at age 60 and older because tax-qualified plans have them paying steep tax penalties if they retire earlier. IULs give you the power to access your money at any age. You are 100% in control of your funds.

11. Protection From Lawsuits (In Many States): Many states protect the cash accumulation inside of the life insurance policy from creditors, lawsuits and judgments. This is a very important benefit for business owners or professionals in high risk professions.

12. Continued Investment If Disabled: The Waiver of Premium for Disability provides policy-holders with the continuation of premium payments that will keep the life insurance in force if they were to become permanently disabled.

13. Does Not Create Taxation Of Social Security Benefits: Based on their income, a large percentage of people are receiving Social Security benefits that can now be subject to income taxation. Regardless of the amounts of the withdrawals, income coming out of a cash-value life insurance policy does not subject an individual's Social Security to income taxation.

14. Avoids Probate: Many people pass away without having properly designating who their valuables are going to, causing numerous problems for their families as it's left to the courts to straighten out the ensuing mess. With an IUL policy, the death benefit is paid directly to the beneficiary or beneficiaries within days of the death of the insured. Additionally, the insured has the ability to have payments made as a lump sum or divide it up over numerous years.

15. Accurate Return Figures: In general returns that are reported by financial products including Whole Life policies are simply smoke and mirrors. IULs performance mirrors either one market or a diversified group where the gains and losses are published in financial periodicals and the internet. Policy holders know exactly what their returns are as a matter of record.

16. Does Not Affect College Financial Aid: Cash Value in life insurance policies are not held against you when you apply for financial aid for your children.

17. Long-Term Care Benefits: An IUL policy can provide Long Term Care needs for just pennies on the dollar if the rider is selected, and the insured is accepted for coverage through underwriting.

Even if you're in your 20's and an Olympic Athlete, read the next chapter. And if you're not an Olympic Athlete, read the next chapter twice. IT'S THAT IMPORTANT!

Read up!

"So many people spend their health gaining wealth, and then have to spend their wealth to regain their health."
— **A. J. Reb Materi**

CHAPTER 22.
THE SKY HIGH COST OF DEPENDENCY.

If you think you should skip over this chapter because it doesn't apply to you, you might just be making a $250,000 mistake.

Most people think that Long Term Care is something that only the elderly will need. The truth of the matter is that 4 out of 10 people will need coverage between the ages of 18 and 64 years old. And 70% of the population will require some services at 65 years and older.

The average annual cost depends on the type and amount of care you receive as well as where you live and the provider you use. The average cost for one year of care in a nursing home is $83,580. In New York it can top $150,000 annually!

And here's the problem: You can spend 20, 30, even 40 years doing everything you can to build up your assets for your future, and then suddenly, you or a loved one needs long term care. And BOOM! Just like that, before you know it, the money starts to drain away. Slowly at first, then faster and faster, until decades of your hard work is wiped away in a matter of two or three years.

It happened to my grandmother. She was living in Florida and her condition had gotten worse so she needed to be in a nursing home. The costs were pretty high, and after a while her bank account was in danger of running dry. So my Mom and Uncle made the painful decision to sell her condo. She wouldn't be going home, and they needed the money to care for her.

That extra money didn't last forever either. Only when Grandma Dora was truly out of money did the government step in and contribute. Yes, you have to be virtually bankrupt and have less than $2,000 in assets before you get financial assistance.

And then the government tells you what facility to go to, how long you stay there and what your level of care is ....

Not a very pretty picture. But the alternative is even worse. I know people that needed to have help taking care of a loved one, but decided to do it on their own. They kept their loved one at home and the family took turns caring for them. What was kind and generous on one hand, became onerous and oppressive. It ended up sucking the life out of everyone surrounding the family member.

People sacrifice their careers, their education, their own health, wealth and sometimes the consequences even breaks up relationships. And that's the saddest part.

A neighbor of mine, Howard, was a very nice man. Loved to bowl. Loved his house. When his health started to go and he needed long term care, his children decided to sell his house. They sold it for $150,000 BELOW MARKET VALUE just to get the cash quickly to take care of their father.

You work a lifetime to build up something, and then seemingly overnight, it's all gone. There has to be a better way to protect against this from happening.

There are Long Term Care insurance policies you can buy. Companies charge you an annual premium based on age and health. Of course, if you're too old or not in good health you can't even qualify for the program. The problem with many of the plans is that they will cost you an arm and leg, and then some.

Every year, you have to pay thousands of dollars in, and just like auto insurance, homeowners insurance, and term insurance, when you don't use it the money is just gone. Every year you need coverage, you have to repeat the payment cycle all over again.

Well, if you take out an IUL policy with a LTC Rider between the ages of 18 and, let's say 75, and can qualify medically for coverage, this is how it can save your bacon.

One: It's affordable. If you take out a policy in your 20s it may only cost you around $10 a month. And if you're in your 40s and 50s and get a policy? It may still only cost you a few hundred dollars annually to get the maximum coverage allowable.

The rules for LTC coverage are set under the Health Insurance Portability and Accounting Act (HIPPA) of 1996. The maximum monthly benefit you can receive is 2% of the face amount (death benefit) on your insurance policy with a daily cap of $330.

What it all boils down to is this: For a low monthly premium you transfer your Long Term Care risk to the insurance company. If and when you need the money down the road, the insurance company will take it out of the death benefit you would leave to your beneficiaries.

For example:

Age	LTC Rider Monthly Cost	Death Benefit:	LTC Protection: 2% up to $330 day
25	$10	$400,000	$8,000 Month
35	$15	$750,000	$9,900 Month
45	$25	$1,500,000	$9,900 Month
55	$35	$1,000,000	$9,900 Month

Depending on the company, LTC costs may differ. To be eligible to receive your benefits, you have to satisfy the following three conditions:
1) Be certified by a Licensed Health Care Practitioner as Chronically Ill, and either:
A) Unable to preform two or more of these Daily Living activities without substantial assistance for an expected period of at least 90 days:
- Bathing
- Continence
- Dressing
- Eating
- Toileting
- Transferring; or

B) The insured has a Severe Cognitive Impairment like dementia or Alzheimer's that requires Substantial Supervision to provide you from health and safety threats.
2) Have an approved plan of care in placement
3) Satisfy the elimination (waiting) period. Usually 90 days.

Once this is done, you can receive checks up to the monthly maximum you're entitled to receive. No receipts are needed, and you can decide how much to take out, and how to apply the money.

You can choose to stay in your home or go to a qualified Long Term Care facility:
- Adult Day Care Center
- Assisted Living
- Hospice Care
- Nursing Home
- Skill Nursing

The point is, you and your family have control of your lives and aren't going to be crushed by the financial burden of Long Term Care ... All because you exercised sound judgment, planned for possibility of it happening, and took the appropriate action to deal with the contingency.

Brilliant!

Now, read on.

"Our goals can only be reached through a vehicle of a plan,
in which we must fervently believe, and upon which we
must vigorously act. There is no other route to success."
— **Stephen A. Brennan**

CHAPTER 23.
THE FOUR FOUNDATION BLOCKS TO
BUILDING A STRONG FINANCIAL FORTRESS.

Have you ever watched the news during a coverage of a storm and they show the aftermath of a devastated neighbor? Debris is everywhere, houses are wrecked. The worst hit are the mobile homes, the trailer parks. Why? They don't have the foundation in place to weather the storm.

The question you have to ask yourself is this: "Am I living in a financial trailer park?" Well, let's find out.

1) Do you have a corner of your financial foundation that gives you the opportunity to earn significant **GROWTH**? Even up to double-digit growth?

2) At the same time you're getting growth do you get **SAFETY**? Heck, anyone can construct a tall building, but adding in all the safety features to protect your interests? That is equally important to ensure your success otherwise it could all come crashing down on your head.

3) You've taken all the time, energy and expense of creating your building, don't you think you should do something to minimum **TAXATION**? Buildings are expensive enough to maintain and operate, you don't want the government tacking on 40% to 50% in additional fees every year, do you?

4) **PROTECTION**. Yep. You build it. Now you need to insure it. Protect it. And make sure it can protect you and your family should anything happen, now or down the road. Including Long Term Care.

Do any of your financial tools give you all four blocks, GROWTH, SAFETY, TAX-ADVANTAGE & PROTECTION?

No?

Then maybe it's time to upgrade to a better location. One where you can build a Financial Fortress that works to give you the solid foundation that can help you achieve your goals and dreams.

THE BUILDING BLOCKS TO A STRONG
FINANCIAL FOUNDATION:

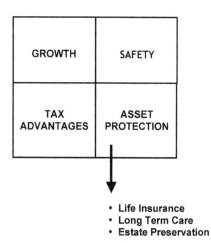

- Life Insurance
- Long Term Care
- Estate Preservation

ACTION ALERT #8:
WATCH THE VIDEO "THE MILLION
DOLLAR GRANDCHILD."

Then read on.

"When it is obvious that the goals cannot be reached,
don't adjust the goals, adjust the action steps."
— **Confucius**

CHAPTER 24.
YOUR OWN PERSONAL FINANCIAL NEEDS ANALYSIS:

It's time to get moving. Remember the X-Curve? Depending on how many responsibilities you've accumulated so far in life, a detailed assessment analysis might be in order.

Knowing where you are, where you want to go, and having the vehicle to get there is key to your success.

A full-scale Financial Needs Analysis targets six main areas:

1. Cashflow
2. Debt Management
3. Emergency Fund
4. Proper Protection
5. Building Wealth
6. Preserve Wealth

Missing from this list are a couple of additional areas that I think are very important to protecting our interests and future financial well-being: Legal matters and Identity Theft Protection. I'll discuss these later in the book.

Most financial planners and advisors are in business to make money for themselves first, and help you second. The preferred method is to perform the "Financial Needs Analysis" in a six-step process:

Step 1. Consultation
Step 2. Fee Collection
Step 3. Information Gathering
Step 4. Analysis
Step 5. Recommendation
Step 6. Sale of Product

For Steps 1-5, fees can range from $500 to $2,500. I once attended a seminar where the presenter charted her method of charging clients. When she first started in the business she charged clients $500 for her clients Financial Needs Analysis.

Quickly she bumped her fee to $700, $800, then $1,000. After speaking with a colleague, she took a deep breath jumped to $2,500. Her reasoning was, "Why not? If there are people out their willing to pay, great!"

When I heard her speak, she was currently charging $9,000 for exactly the same analysis she did when she was charging $500. Wow. I guess that's one way to "help" people. To me it's more like the Placebo Effect in medicine. You give someone a sugar pill, tell them it's medicine, and they get better. Maybe some people feel they are getting better service when they spend a lot of money.

On the other hand, maybe that's why some surveys show that 75% of the population has never met with a Financial Advisor.

How about this? As you know, my Mission is education. I think we have major problems in this country (and in the world) because good, solid, practical knowledge is not provided to people in way that they can absorb it, use it and share it with others. My not-for-profit educational organization www.16ThingsKidsCanDo.Org is designed to work on changing this.

Now, what's this have to do with you? By reading this book, you are demonstrating that you interested enough to want to learn, and do some things better for yourself, and your family.

I will give you your custom Personal Needs Analysis for free. That's eliminating Step #2 and replacing it with Free Financial Education. The kind that Banks, Wall Street and most financial advisors don't want you to know, or charge you up the whazoo whether they teach it or not.

I will still provide Steps #1, #3, and #4.

I will replace Steps #5 and Step #6 with Custom Recommendations

I will add Step #8 and Deliver the best program from best product provider to meet your goals.

I will add Step #9. Family Legal Advice options.

I will add Step #10. Individual and Family Identity Theft protection options.

I will add Steps #11 & #12. This gives you income earning options.

Now, if you are learning something and benefiting in some way from what I am sharing, the only thing I would appreciate you to do in return is recommend my book and our services to others!

ACTION ALERT #9:
PLAYING IT FORWARD

Go on-line and complete the Action Alert and the Workbook, and you'll have another piece of your financial puzzle completed.

ON-LINE WORKBOOK #4:
YOUR OWN PERSONAL FINANCIAL NEEDS ANALYSIS

Then, coming up shortly is one of the key ingredients to making it all happen. We're in the home stretch and I can't wait for you to get there. After you complete a workbook or two.

Click. Click.

Summary of steps my experienced licensed financial team provides.

Free Services:

Step 1. Consultation

Step 2. Education

Step 3. Information Gathering

Step 4. Strength of Selection

Step 5. Analysis

Step 6. Custom Recommendation

Step 7. Custom Illustration

Step 8. Delivery of Best Policy

Additional Programs:

Step 9. Legal Advice Options

Step 10. Identity Theft Protection Options

Step 11. Additional Income Options

Step 12. Additional Business Ownership Options

"Family is not an important thing. It's everything."
— **Michael J. Fox**

CHAPTER 25.
PROTECTING YOUR WHY:
THE D.I.M.E. METHOD.

Remember, what we said about you being a ATM machine for your family? And if something were to happen to you, what would that do to your family financially?

Well, a lot of clients ask me: "What is the right amount of insurance or protection to have?" "Do I have too much? Do I have too little? Do I have just the right amount?"

So one of the things I am going to show you is a method I use to identify the right amount of insurance for each individual. When you use this method, you'll know you're not going to get more insurance than you really need, or if somebody comes around later ,and tells you need more than you have.

It's called the DIME method, and it's an acronym that stands for:

D	=	Debt
I	=	Income
M	=	Mortgage
E	=	Education

So these areas are some of the major expenses you are taking care of. Right now while you are alive, you handling all the debt, providing the income for the family, handling the mortgage or rent, and you are setting aside money for educational expenses of your children.

Even if you don't have any children yet, the earlier to start setting money aside in the right place, the more you will have available when they need it, and the less painful and stressful it will be in the long run.

Now, if something, God forbid, was to happen to you, who is going to handle these responsibilities? Who is going to step in and pay for your responsibilities? The company or place where you work? Nope. Your family? Probably not. Your friends? Don't think so.

But you can transfer this risk to an insurance company, and they will. And this is something you absolutely should do, and this is how we are going to handle it:

Let's start with your children's education. "Do you want your kids go to a good college if you pass away?" Many times I hear from the parents: "Sure, I want my kids to go. But I want them to pay for it themselves. That will teach them a lesson, and they can learn something from it."

And that is true; if you were alive that might be a great opportunity to have your kids learn that lesson. But for me, I don't want my kids dealing with my passing away, plus the struggle of going to college. It's too much for them to have to handle, and it could ruin their own lives.

I want to have this covered when I'm alive, just in case, so they can get to college, not have to worry, and do something bigger and better by themselves.

So "Where do you want them to go? A state school or a private school?" Lets say you have two children, and it costs $40,000 per year per child to get them educated. That is pretty simple math. We are talking now about $160,000 each, or $320,000.

EDUCATION   = $ 320,000

Next up, your mortgage. You have a 30-year mortgage with 22 number of years still left on the books. Your monthly payment is $1,843. Your annual payment is $22,116. Now, multiply your annual amount by a factor of 10. You can round the total up if you like: $230,000. This should effectively take care of your mortage.

MORTGAGE   = $ 230,000

Add up all your miscellaneous debt: Car and student loans, credit cards, etc. How much money would it take to wipe the slate clean?

DEBT   = $ 83,200

Now ask yourself the question, "How much money do you want to have come in when the mortgage is paid off, education is handled and you are out of debt? What do you want have come in just to supplement the income for your family?"

Remember the ATM example? Let's look at what you're replacing. Say it's $5,000 a month, $60,000 for the year.

Okay, how long do you want that income coming in for? What period of time? 10 years? 20 years? Or do you want it to come in forever? If your answer is 10 years, simply multiply the replacement amount by 10. $600,000.

But let's say the answer is "Forever." This is how you figure that out. It's a simple mathematical equation, but it is kinda cool. So pay extra special attention.

Let's assume for a minute you had a million dollars, and you were earning 6% interest. I know the interest is around 1% for a high yield CD right now. But with that amount of cash, you can go on the market and get a guarantee of 5% or 6% from one of the companies.

So, a million dollars generating 6% interest would be your $60,000 a year, and $5,000 a month. All you have to do is use that bucket of a million dollars and figure out what interest you need to get to get you to the amount you want to replace.

Remember the key to the X-Curve is not how much you make, but being able to live off the interest your assets generate. You don't want the principal to be exhausted over time.

$$\textbf{INCOME} \quad = \quad \$1,000,000$$

Now, all we have to do is add it up:

$$
\begin{array}{lcl}
\textbf{D} & = & \$\quad 83,200 \\
\textbf{I} & = & \$\ 1,000,000 \\
\textbf{M} & = & \$\quad 230,000 \\
\textbf{E} & = & \$\quad 320,000
\end{array}
$$

If this were your situation, the total amount of insurance coverage you would need would be about $1,500,000. - $1,600,000. And now you know how to calculate your insurance needs.

But knowledge is not enough, right? You still have to Act to get things done.

ON-LINE WORKBOOK #5:
IT'S TIME FOR YOUR DIME.

And the fact that you did something about it and made the choice to offset that risk for a just pennies on the dollar, should be very comforting to you and your family.

Just like what's coming up next ...

Read on!

"It is not only what we do, but also what
we do not do, for which we are accountable."
— **Moliere**

CHAPTER 26.
THE IMPORTANCE OF PAYING YOURSELF FIRST
(OR THE MOST OVER-LOOKED OR IGNORED
CONCEPT YOU MAY HAVE NEVER LEARNED
FROM YOUR $200,000 COLLEGE EDUCATION)

As we talked about earlier in the concept "The Big Zero" most people end up spending their monthly income on the big three: Living expenses, debt and taxes. Now, I'm going to show you the importance of paying yourself first, and how that can make a huge impact on whether you reach your goal of financial independence.

Let's say you're 25 years old, unmarried, and renting a small apartment on your own. You know that in the future you're going to get married, buy a house, and have kids. So, you, Mr. Proactive, decide to get a jump on your retirement planning by putting away $10 a day or $300 a month.

Now, let's say you're getting an 8% return on your money. Looking at the chart below, we're just going to show the first seven years of what you pay in. Now we fast forward to when you're 48 years old: Your account will have grown to over a $128,000.

At the same time you started to contribute to your fund, you had a friend that you went to college with, Mr. Procrastinator. Mr. Procrastinator decided he wanted to spend a little more on a car, party a little more, before he started his retirement fund. After all, he reasoned, he wasn't married, and he wasn't earning that much after college.

So at age 32, Mr. Procrastinator finally started to put away the same $10 a day, $300 dollars a month as you did. Just to reach the same amount as you have at age 48, Mr. Procrastinator had to pay $3,600 more a year for an additional TEN YEARS!

Now, at 48 years old, you both have around $130,000 in your respective accounts, but let's look at the total contribution that you put in versus what Mr. Procrastinator put in.

Your contribution was only $25,200. Mr. Procrastinator had to contribute almost two and a half times as much $61,200!

The High Cost Of Waiting					
MR. PROACTIVE			MR. PROCRASTINATION		
Age:	Yearly Contribution:	Total Accumulation:	Age:	Yearly Contribution:	Total Accumulation:
25	$3,600	$3,888	25	$0	$0
26	$3,600	$8,087	26	$0	$0
27	$3,600	$12,622	27	$0	$0
28	$3,600	$17,520	28	$0	$0
29	$3,600	$22,809	29	$0	$0
30	$3,600	$28,522	30	$0	$0
31	$3,600	$34,692	31	$0	$0
32	$0	$37,467	32	$3,600	$3,888
33	$0	$40,465	33	$3,600	$8,087
34	$0	$43,702	34	$3,600	$12,622
35	$0	$47,198	35	$3,600	$17,520
36	$0	$50,974	36	$3,600	$22,809
37	$0	$55,052	37	$3,600	$28,522
38	$0	$59,456	38	$3,600	$34,692
39	$0	$64,212	39	$3,600	$41,355
40	$0	$69,349	40	$3,600	$48,552
41	$0	$74,897	41	$3,600	$56,324
42	$0	$80,889	42	$3,600	$64,718
43	$0	$87,360	43	$3,600	$73,783
44	$0	$94,349	44	$3,600	$83,574
45	$0	$101,897	45	$3,600	$94,148
46	$0	$110,048	46	$3,600	$105,567
47	$0	$118,852	47	$3,600	$117,901
48	$0	$128,361	48	$3,600	$131,221
TOTAL CASH CONTRIBUTION:			TOTAL CASH CONTRIBUTION:		
$25,200			$61,200		
*10X's: $225,200 = $1,283,610 Total			*10X's: $612,000 = $1,312,210 Total		

*Starting Early Saved Mr. Proactive $358,200

It gets worse for Mr. Procrastinator. imagine if you add another 0 on the end of those figures? Imagine if you had contributed 10x's the money in your account: $250,200. You retirement would have grown to $1,283,610. You'd be pretty happy, yes?

How about Mr. Procrastinator? He would have had to contribute $610,200 to reach the same level. That's $360,000 more.

And this is the power of starting early and paying yourself first. It's one of the few concepts in this book that colleges teach to their finance and economics students.

The fancy name for it is … "The Time Value Relationship of Money."

You can use that to impress your friends. And you can start early and pay yourself first, and impress your family.

Even if you can't start at 25 years old, 35 years old or 45 years old … it doesn't matter. The main point is that once you know about this concept, you take advantage of it, and be Mr. Proactive.

Now, this is such an important concept, let me share another way to look at this. Let's say you wanted to build your nest egg up to a million dollars. Assuming you're earning 8% interest and you don't have taxes, 1) how much would you have to put away monthly, and (2) for how long would you have to do it to reach your goal?

Let's look at the numbers:

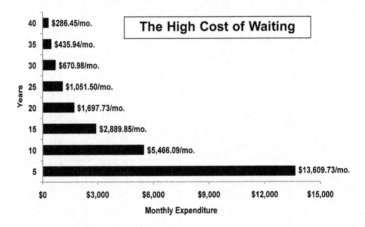

What this means is that you can save yourself hundreds of thousands of dollars by starting as soon as possible and letting the power of compound interest do the heavy lifting for you.

And it's never to late to add to your income so that you have the money to catch-up later on in life. Read on!

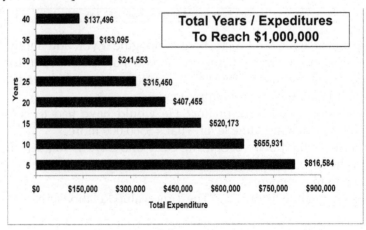

SECTION IV:
THE SECRET TO YOUR SUCCESS.

PART II:
ROBERT KIYOSAKI

"You see, in life, lots of people know what to do,
but few people actually do what they know.
Knowing is not enough! You must take action."
— **Anthony Robbins**

"Oh, people don't even know. If poor people knew how rich rich people are, there would be riots in the streets."
— **Chris Rock**

CHAPTER 27.
INCOME INEQUALITY: THE RICH GET RICHER & WHY YOUR LEGACY SUCKS.

There has been a lot of talk recently about income inequality in the media lately. How out of whack things have become. But this type of talk has been going on for a very long time.

The ice cream company, Ben & Jerry's often stated mission was to provide great ice cream for its customers while providing a great place to work for its employees. The way they did that was having a policy that the highest paid employee's (Chief Operating Officer Chuck Lacy earned $150,000) salary shall not be more than five times greater than an entry-level employee earning $12 an hour.

Never mind the fact that the math didn't quite add up ($12 an hour is $24,000 annually. $24,000 x 5 = $120,000), the company quickly scrapped the policy when it needed to find a new CEO later that same year. No potential CEO was willing to work under the ratio.

Most Americans think the ideal ratio should be 7-to-1. Their best guess is that it's more likely 30-to-1. As for reality? Would you belive it's 354-to-1?

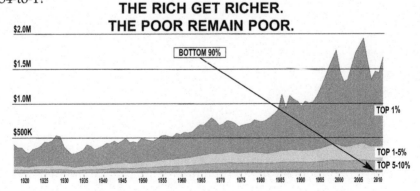

THE RICH GET RICHER.
THE POOR REMAIN POOR.

The average wage earner makes annually? $35,000. Meanwhile the average CEO package is worth is $15 million! Since 1978, employees earning power has risen 11%. CEO wages have increased 1,000 percent!

We'd like to believe we can work hard and become rich, but the numbers don't bear it out:

	% Of Wealth: Top 20%:	% Of Wealth: Bottom 40%:
Americans Believe:	59%	9%
Reality Sucks:	84%	3%
Walton (Walmart) Family:	> Wealth	42% Of All Americans

	% of Americans:	% of Wealth:
The TOP:	20%	84%
The MIDDLE:	40%	13%
The BOTTOM:	40%	3%

According to a recent article in Scientific American, the United States is now the most financially polarized country out of all Western nations. And we have less social mobility than Canada and Europe.

I don't know about you, but these numbers make my stomach churn. There is something fundamentally wrong here that we shouldn't just accept. We owe it to ourselves, our families and our future to do something for ourselves and others to close the gap.

It's not going to happen by itself.

It's not going to happen because the rich have a change of heart.

It's not going to happen because politicians see the "light."

It's not going to happen if you don't decide to make it happen.

So read on!

WHY THE 99 PERCENTERS NEED A RAISE

"Oh, you hate your job? Why didn't you say so? There's a support group for that. It's called EVERYBODY, and they meet at the bar."
— **Drew Carey**

CHAPTER 28.
HOW DO YOU MAKE YOUR MONEY? E? S? B? I?

If you've been around long enough, chances are you've heard of the book "Rich Dad, Poor Dad" by Robert Kiyosaki. Kiyosaki studied how his father, a University professor, worked, earned and lived, and then compared it to how his best friend's father, a business owner, did those same things.

Over the course of many years, Kiyosaki made some rather keen observations and judgments. One of these observations he named "The Cashflow Quadrant."

Kiyosaki concluded that it doesn't matter what your background is, what education you have, where you are from, or even how much money you make ... everyone who earns money can be put into one of four quadrants.

The Cashflow Quadrant

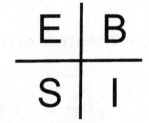

E = EMPLOYEES: About 90% of the population are "E" people. Employees. These 90% work for the other 10%. And as an employee what you are really doing is making your boss's goals and dreams become a reality.

You trade your time for a little bit of money, but you'll never truly become financially independent by being an employee. If you work for somebody else you are not financially independent. You are making those people's goals and dreams happen. They are the ones that are on vacations on their yachts, and enjoying themselves in Hawaii while you are still punching your time card.

As an employee you have someone else telling you how much your worth: $30,000, $50,000 or even $100,000 a year. You might feel that you are worth much, much more, but not to the company you work for.

So as an employee ...

• You don't control how much you're paid
• You don't control your raises (read more at the end of the chapter)
• You don't control the hours that you work
• You don't control your vacations. You have to ask permission to go on vacation
• You don't even control whether you have a job six months down the line, let alone two or three years down the road

S = SMALL BUSINESS OWNERS: Some employees get fed up with that situation and they decide to become small business owners. These are real estate agents, doctors, dentists, lawyers, shop owners, restaurant owners, etc.

As a small business owner you have the opportunity to make a lot more money than employees, but you also take on a lot more responsibility.

Let's say you own a restaurant. You might be working 16 hours a day, seven days a week — literally 365 days a year. And what's true of employees and a lot of small business owners is that once you stop work, your income is over.

That's why the restaurant owner doesn't want to leave the restaurant, because they know that when they come back they might not have the same business as when they left.

I was a small business owner since I was in college at University of Florida. Years later, I sold my printing and design company so I could move to New York city to pitch the magazine I created. I was successful at producing my magazine, but not so successful at selling my business.

Within a year the person I sold to decided to stop paying me. I was up in New York working a hundred and ten hours a week on my magazine. So what was I going to do, stop everything and go down to Florida and argue with the guy over a few thousand dollars a month? I let it go. Later, I was able to get the equipment back, and that was the end of it.

B = BIG BUSINESS OWNERS: So some people want to be on the big business side of the quadrant, and generally what they do is buy franchises. This is your McDonalds, Subways, State Farms, Century 21s, etc.

Do you know how much it costs to buy a McDonalds franchise? Up to $2,000,000! And then you have to go to Hamburger University for a year. Really, how long does it take to learn how to cook a frozen hamburger or frozen french fries? Maybe five minutes?

So what they are learning? It's the business system. Because it's the system that makes them successful, not really the food. The food kind of sucks when you compare it to going to a diner right next door. You can spend a couple of dollars more and you're getting a lot better food. But people know that they can go to New York, Georgia and California and they're going to get the same service, the same quality of food and the same experience, and they like that.

So what he says if you want to become wealthy you need to be in the right hand sight of the quadrant. The problem is that the most people don't have hundreds of thousands, let alone million dollars to invest.

The reason why it's very attractive to be in the B-Quarter business is because these businesses have proven systems that work. Whether or not you are average, smart, handsome or not, you work the system, and the system will work and make you money. The system is the best method to "Save Yourself Time Energy & Money" in the pursuit of your goals.

So it doesn't matter whether the franchise owner was a truck driver or Harvard MBA when they go through hamburger University. When they come out they can be equally successful. Because it's the business system that makes them successful.

Think about it. When you go to McDonalds do you ever see the owner there? Nope. They are the wealthy, the 10%, they plug people into the system. 16 years old kids run the system. 65 year olds run the system.

They know what to make, when to make it, how to make it. Everything looks the same, the number one is still a Big Mac. They give out free food, they drop food, the food doesn't taste really good, but it still makes money.

The owners profit share on the work that employees do. And that's how they make their money.

I = INVESTMENTS: Now the last thing that Kiyosaki says is that everyone, regardless of where they are on the cashflow quadrant — employees, small business owners, or big business owners, — everyone needs to be doing something for their retirement, for his or her savings and investments.

And what Kiyosaki is saying in "The Cashflow Quadrant" is 100% on point with my organizations goals and dreams.

Our Educational Mission:

1) **Helping People To Properly Build For Their Future:** We take people who are employees, small business owners, big business owners and move them over to the savings and investment portion of the quadrant in order to get better returns on their money, tax-free, just like the rich.

2) **Helping People Become Financially Independent Through Big Business Ownership:** We also take employees and small business owners and we move them over to the big business side of the equation where they can earn money in the financial services industry by using a proven business system that has helped hundreds of thousands of individuals and families over the years become financially independent.

> "The richest people in the world look for and build networks; everyone else looks for work."
> — **Robert Kiyosaki**

A Little More On Being An Employee:

I give career talks to graduating college and university classes, and if the school's Career Resource Directory is sitting in on the talk, I always make it a point to ask her, "What is the typical amount of a raise someone would get working in corporate America?"

The answer I almost always get back is this: "If they get a raise, it would be either one, two or three percentage of their annual salary."

So, let's break this down. If you are making 50,000 dollars a year working for a company, your 3 percent raise will gross you 1,500 dollars. Now, take out your taxes, and you have around 1,000 left. Divide that by 12, and you getting paid about 83 dollars a month.

You know what you can do with that 83 dollars a month? You can go to dinner, go to a movie, and buy a jumbo bucket of popcorn. The only problem is, you're going alone. You can't afford to take anyone with you.

And that is the sad state of being an employee in corporate America. Read on!

"Constantly having to think about money is not nice. People used
to say, 'Being rich doesn't make you happy'. And I'd think,
'I've got no electricity, nothing — tell that to my empty fridge'."
— Rebecca Ferguson

CHAPTER 29.
A NEW KIND OF EMPLOYEE BENEFITS PLAN:
HOW TO BECOME FINANCIALLY INDEPENDENT
WITHOUT GETTING A RAISE.

Millions of Americans work for companies that have no retirement program. While millions more may already have a retirement plan through
a 401(k) or 403(b).

Regardless of your company's program, or lack of one, you need to
share this program with management, human resources, the owners.
It's good for you and it's good for them. A true "Win Win."

Winner #1. You. At a minimum you get a retirement plan that gives
you the Financial Foundation benefits:

    1) Growth

    2) Safety

    3) Tax Advantages

    4) Protection

The company can contribute, or not, to your plan through a custom
Matching program or a set monthly, quarterly or annual amount. You
can also arrange to have Bonuses paid directly into your retirement
account. Finally, tt's 100% portable. Meaning you can leave the company, and immediately take it with you.

Winner #2. Your Company or Organization: If you're happy about
how your company respects you, and cares about your future well-
being ... then you will work better, stay longer, and be more loyal to the
company.

Our organization's Retirement Benefits Program is 100% free to your
company. It costs you:

    1) Nothing to Set-Up

    2) Nothing to Administer

    3) Nothing to Create Flexible Contribution Schedules

You can also have them visit our website, **www.MyESBN.com,** for more information on the program. And of, course, there is the old standby, the phone call: 212 213-0257!

"People clinging to job security, savings, retirement plans, and other relics will be the ones financially-ravaged from 2010-2020, the most volatile world-changing decade in history."
— **Robert Kiyosaki**

CHAPTER 30.
IN THE LAND OF THE GIG ECONOMY
THE BIG BUSINESS OPPORTUNITY.

The economic upheavals that this country has experienced over the last two generations has changed more than business attitudes toward their employees. Since 1937, the Fair Labor Standards Act set the maximum workweek at 40 hours, and provided that employees who worked more than the maximum would receive an overtime bonus.

To get around this many companies "promoted" workers into meaningless "titled" management positions (think Vice Presidents at banks) so employees could work more than the 40 hours per week without triggering time and half overtime wage increases.

Other companies chronically under employed staff by limiting the number of hours employees could work per week to less than full time. This way the company could avoid contributing to person's employment benefits like health care or retirement.

These situations coupled with numerous others including high unemployment, stagnant wages, high taxation, lack of good-paying jobs, worker dissatisfaction, the high cost of child care, etc. has led many people to embrace a different kind of employment model: That of the Gig Worker.

Gigs (or jobs) used to be the domain of the working musician that would line up work and travel from one "Gig" to the next. The word migrated into securing jobs in other fields as well, and it become synonymous with work done by freelancers. Work done by individuals who had more flexibility and control over their daily lives than their counterparts, "employees."

But what workers seemingly acquire in managing their own lives, they often lose in health, retirement and vacation benefits.

None-the-less, the Gig workforce is steadily expanding. People that once held traditional jobs have opted out by choice or necessity. Day laborers, graphic designers, house cleaners, web designers, writers, dog walkers, life coaches, marketers, personal chef, tutors … and the list goes on and on.

But it's not only individuals that are randomly moving into the market. Entire new industries are being build to take advantage of the Gig worker. The most famous one is the car service, Uber.

Uber was created in 2009 to offer an alternative transportation option for people taking taxicabs. Now, through Uber people can hire individuals using their own cars. Today, the company operates in 58 countries and 300 cities worldwide. As of the beginning of 2015, Uber had 162,037 active drivers that had completed four or more trips for customers. And that number is doubling every six months. By 2016, the number of drivers is expected to exceed 1,000,000!

The flexibility and control workers have over their own schedules, circumstances and interests are the biggest pros the gig economy has going for it.

The biggest con, aside from the lack of health insurance, vacation time, retirement plans, is the lack of consistent work over a long period of time. Freelancers often earn more money hourly than employees, but don't put in the same number of hours week after week, month after month. These gaps in "billable hours" often lead to less overall income for workers.

The real estate industry has over 2.5 million agents and brokers that are essentially freelancers. Freelancers that operate under the same pros and cons as members of the gig economy. 10% of the agents make 90% of the money, and 90% of all agents fail in the business. The serious money is made by the brokers.

Remember, Robert Kiyosaki's Cashflow Quadrant that shows how people earn their money? Brokers are on the Big Business side of the equation along with the McDonalds owner. A Broker plugs agents into his or her real estate system, and then profit shares with them on listings, rentals and sales.

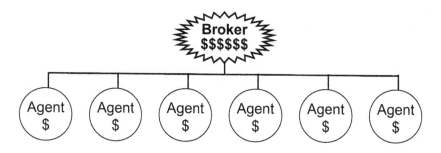

Agents have the opportunity to earn large paydays, but just like employees, once they stop working, it's game over – their income stops. One the other side of the equation, the Broker is the one that is making the big bucks by profit sharing with all the agents out the field. And just like McDonalds owners, brokers put up the capital to open and run the business, but they make their money without having to do sales themselves.

Brokers can take time off and still have their incomes continue. They have the opportunity to earn "Massive, Passive Income" due to their system and the efforts of their agents.

And as Robert Kiyosaki has shone, operating a business under this type of business system is where you want to be if you want to be on the Big Business side of the quadrant, just like the rich.

Now, in the Financial Services industry, some company's have Agents (called Associates) that come in to the industry, on a part-time or full-time basis, get trained and licensed for a fraction of the cost of Real Estate agents, help people, and earn significant income just like a real estate Broker.

Bloomberg Financial News conducted an analysis of **the top careers with the highest income potential** based on the U.S. Bureau of Labor Statistics' Occupational Employment Statistics. Number one on the list?

#1. **Securities, Commodities and Financial Services Sales Agents:**
The top 10% earned over $159,276, and the bottom 10% made less than $30,948.

#2. **Athletes and Sports Competitors:**
The top 10% earned over $94,504, and the bottom 10% made less than $20,708.

#3. **Real Estate Brokers:**
The top 10% earned over $116,203, and the bottom 10% earned less than $26,548.

#4. **Personal Financial Advisors:**
The top 10% earned over $141,350, and the bottom 10% earned less than $33,412.

What's interesting is that two of the top four professions are in the financial services industry. And, if you're looking to earn extra income, or replace your full-time earnings with something that can double or triple your current earnings – all while helping others – then this might be a good business for you.

Read on.

"The best thing about being rich is the freedom;
freedom to do whatever you want,
whenever you want. It doesn't suck."
— **Tommy Lee**

CHAPTER 31.
A TOP-RATED PROFESSIONAL CAREER IN 30-DAYS & BIG BUSINESS OWNERSHIP FOR LESS THAN IT COSTS TO HAVE A NIGHT ON THE TOWN.

If you think of the jobs that earn the most money, what comes to mind first? Doctors and lawyers, right? Doctors. Eight to 12 years of college. Lawyers, seven years.

Now, as we just saw, Financial Advisors are right up there in earnings. And it doesn't take seven to 12 years of college. It doesn't take four years either. The professionals are government regulated and licensed. And it can be done in less than 30 days.

That doesn't mean you're an expert. It simply means you can start earning income. There are three main areas of licensing life, health and securities. And my organization has programs designed to get you trained, licensed, and on track to helping people through personal mentoring, group, team and field training.

And once you're licensed, there are three ways you can earn income:

#1. Referrals: You know people that would benefit from our services, but you can't take the time to help them personally. Simply refer them, and you'll earn 50% of what you would ordinarily earn helping people personally.

#2. Personal or Direct: You've learned the ropes, you know how to assess people's needs and goals, and do the necessary analysis and illustrations to give your clients the best plans to help them achieve their objectives.

#3. Management/Ownership: Just like a real estate broker, you bring people into your organization, help them grow and develop, and share in the profits whether or not you are doing client work personally.

The great thing about what we do is, we get to help people based on what's important to them, not to one particular company. We are Mission driven. Not commission driven. We work with an independent financial broker/dealer, and we are 100% free to recommend any one of over 100 companies that are suitable for our clients.

We work with old, established multi-billion companies that you are already familiar with: Nationwide, Prudential, Transamerica, Voya, Fidelity, Wells Fargo, Goldman Sachs, and dozens more. We bring our clients financial education that other companies and institutions don't want them to know, and then provide them with the best option to achieve their goals.

We are like a financial supermarket with five aisles representing the five areas where we work: Protection; Annuities; Stocks, Bonds, Mutual funds; Retirement Plans; and Long Term Care. And just like in a supermarket on each of these aisles there are dozens of companies with hundreds of products available.

So, here's what we provide for our clients:
1) A Financial Education On How Money Works
   & How To Get Money To Work Hard For Yourself
2) Free Financial Needs Analysis
3) Mission Over Commission Philosophy & Action
4) "Strength In Selection"
5) The Best Options To Meet Their Needs
6) Clients Never Pay Extra For Our Services
7) Free Reviews Of Insurance Policies, Retirement Plans & Securities

When clients pay for a plan we recommend, they don't pay us. They pay directly to the company we recommend, and that company pays us, in advance, out of future profit.

And that is very cool. For clients and for us. So, for illustration purposes, I'm going to give you a couple of examples of how this can work.

Illustration #1. Family of Four. Husband, Wife, two children. Both parents work, are renters, and want to give their children a great head start in life. They decide to set-up protection and retirement plans for everyone. The adults qualify for $750,000 in life insurance protection; $9,800 a month in Long Term Care Protection, and are building up their tax-free retirement accounts at the same time. For their children, they have $250,000 in protection on each, and are also building up their cash value accounts to give to them when they graduate from college or get married.

For all of this, the total amount the family would pay in on a monthly basis might only be $833. That's $10,000 annually. Because of the growth, safety, tax and protection benefits – it's an unbeatable combination. And as an Associate who helped them understand and secure the plans, you earn a percentage of the gross amount they paid in based on the first year.

Depending on what state your client is from (you need to be licensed in that state, too) you would earn 35% or 45% of that $10,000. The client doesn't pay it. The multi-billion dollar company that you recommend, and the client accepts, pay your fees. And they pay it in advance out of future earnings. Here's how it works.

When the client illustration you provided is accepted by the client, and the first month premium paid, you'll receive 40% of your earnings within a week or so. Meanwhile, the client gets their free check-up and goes through the underwriting process to determine suitability for coverage. Clients still have to get approved. Once approved, you will receive the policy and deliver it personally to the client. When client accepts the policy and signs for it, you send that in and within a week or two you receive the remaining 60% of your earnings.

The entire process might take four or five hours, and your earnings would be $3,500 at 35%. But that's not all, every year your client pays into their account you earn residual income, a small percentage of what they pay in. And clients pay into their retirement accounts for 20, 30, even 40 years!

That's massive, passive income. That's your own pension plan. But earning 35% is only the first step. Depending on how well you do helping clients, you can earn promotions that increase your earning percentages. Imagine doing the same amount of work and earning $4,500, $5,000, even $6,500 for just a few hours work?

We are in the money business. We get to earn Wall Street money for helping our clients. And we are not limited to where we can help, or how many we can help.

I have a neighbor that is in my company. He owns a house one block from ocean, earns over $100,000 per year, and works only around 10 hours a month. He has everything he wants in life. A tremendous home, a great wife. And he doesn't want to work hard. He has no children that he wants to leave a legacy for, so for him this is the perfect situation.

On the other hand, I have people in my organization that are much, much more ambitious. And that brings me to the third way you can earn income:

Ask yourself this question, "How many hours a day can you work to be earning money?" Think of your answer. If your answer was 8 hours a day, you think like an employee. People that think like managers say 10-12 hours a day. And business owners think 24 hours a day.

Rich Big Business Owners think like this: "I can earn money 24/7. But wouldn't it be smarter to profit share with 10 "24/7" People? Then you have 240 hours in a day where you could be earning money, yes?
Well ...

#3. Management/Ownership: This is the Big Business path to ownership. Imagine being able to share the business income opportunity with friends, relatives, co-workers and associates. What a difference it could make in their lives having the ability to earn an extra thousand or two or three a month. I'm willing to bet it would make a huge difference giving them the ability to pay off debt, pay down mortgages, and properly fund retirements.

All because you took the first step and decided to do something positive for your own future. And now you have the ability, and the responsibility of helping others as well.

Now, let's say you worked hard, followed our business system. You earned your promotions, and six months, a year down the road, you are now a Senior Marketing Director in our firm, earning the highest level of client compensation the company pays. In New York, that is 65%, outside of New York, it's 81%.

In addition to what you earn directly or personally, you have the ability to earn the difference between your compensation level and your associates. So, if you are at 65% and your training associate is at 25%, and the client pays in, for illustration purposes, $10,000 annually, the company pays out 65% or $6,500. Your training associate, assuming they are licensed, earns 25% or $2,500, and you earn the difference 40% or $4,000.

Look at it this way: If you had five clients or families that each paid in $833 a month/$10,000 annually, this is the compensation you would earn:

Position:	Associate Earnings:		Your SMD Earnings:	
Training Associate:	25%	$2,500	40%	$4,000
Associate:	35%	$3,500	30%	$3,000
Senior Associate:	45%	$4,500	20%	$2,000
Marketing Director:	50%	$5,000	15%	$1,500
Senior Marketing Director:	0%	$ -0-	65%	$6,500

Your total compensation for the month? $17,000. And, you are not limited to four associates or five clients. You are free to help people throughout the United States, Canada and Puerto Rico. The more associates you help become successful the more they are able to reach out and help others, and the more you are fulfilling the Mission of the company.

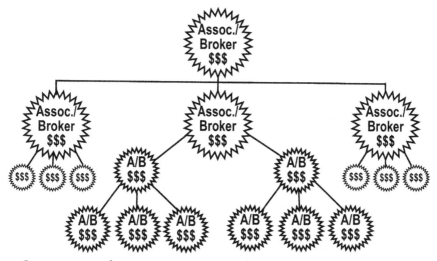

Once you reach Senior Marketing Director, you're on your way to earning over $100,000 annually. Three years later, you have ownership of the ID the company assigned you when you first started. You can sell it for 10 times your annual income. If you're earning $150,000 annually, you could sell your business for $1.5 million. And that's how much your net worth has increased, because you came into the business.

From Zero to Hero. It's all up to you. No one is going to give you $100,000 just because you're good-looking. We're not a modeling agency. You have to put in the time and work for it. While you're learning, you're overworked and underpaid. How quickly you move to overpaid and underworked, is up to you.

We will do everything we can to give you to the tools and skills to help you be successful. But believe me when I tell you that your success has nothing to do with how educated, smart or creative you are. It has everything to do with these three things:

The Secret To Your Success:
#1. Desire: You have to have a burning desire to change your live and the lives of others.
#2. Determination: You have to make strong commitment and follow through. You must give yourself a minimum of six months to learn and earn.
#3. Coach-ability: We have a proven system for success that if you follow, you will be successful. Follow your leaders, follow your trainer, and follow the business format system. Our goal is to make you successful, for only then we are successful too.
     Read on.

"Nothing happens until something moves."
— **Sir John Denham**

CHAPTER 32.
THE TIME TO ACT IS NOW.

In the previous chapters I hope you've learned a quite a bit about what it takes to make your money work hard for you. Now comes the moment of truth.

What are you going to do to get your money to work hard for you? It's not enough that you've acquired some knowledge. You need to act on that knowledge and apply it. You don't want to find yourself worse off in the future because you didn't act.

So what are your options?
1. Ask for your free consultation
2. Ask for your free analysis and custom illustration
3. Ask about getting on the path to earning more income

ACTION ALERT #10.
THE TIME TO ACT IS NOW.

The Time To Change Your Life Is Now!

"I started off with a company, InfoSpace, with my own funding. The company was listed among the most successful companies and I went on to start Intelius and Moon Express. Now, I focus my time on using the skills of an entrepreneur to solve many of the grand challenges facing us in the areas of education, healthcare, clean water and energy."
— **Naveen Jain**

"Incredible change happens in your life when you decide to take control of what you do have power over instead of craving control over what you don't."
— **Steve Maraboli**

CHAPTER 33.
EITHER YOU PLAN FOR THE FUTURE
OR YOU PLAN TO FAIL.

You want to earn 6-figure residual income? Well, to get to where you want to go you need a plan. And you need to work your plan. In the early 1950s there was a study done at one of the Ivy league schools where researchers interviewed graduating students to see how many had created a business plan for their future. Only 3% of the class had a plan. The remaining 97% were driving to Florida with no map and no GPS. Figuratively, of course.

Twenty years later the researchers interviewed everyone that was still alive. It turned out that the 3% that had created business plans before graduating were much wealthier than the other 97% – combined!

It's that simple.

This is not a 70-page business plan for a start-up company. This is a highly individual and personal business plan that targets multiple areas you need to develop and strengthen inside yourself in order to achieve your goals and dreams.

Detailed below is a format for a business plan that has been successfully used to help thousands of people in a leading financial services company.

After the sample, I compiled a list of Affirmations that you can choose from to help you develop your own plan in the next chapter. And of course, you'll be able to use your on-line workbook to help you along the way.

Don't worry if you don't have the confidence in how you're going to achieve your financial goals and dreams. That will come in time, especially once you're open to the possibilities and you're developing the proper mindset for you to get there.

SAMPLE BUSINESS & LIFE PLAN:

OPENING STATEMENT: This is the year for changing my future by changing who I am. Learning as much as I can and building as fast as I can to control the outcome of my future.

AFFIRMATIONS:
- I am positive
- My dreams will become reality
- I love helping others
- I am persistent
- I am a leader
- I am coachable

TOP REASONS:
- I want to retire my parents so they can enjoy their life
- I want to pay off our debt so we can move forward with our dreams
- I want to start having children
- I want to have a great lifestyle

PERSONAL:
- I will tell my family "I love you" & "I appreciate you" everyday
- I will not waste time on computer games and TV
- I will be more open with my family and share how I feel
- I will stand up for my beliefs and not be swayed by what others say

PHYSICAL:
- I will exercise everyday for at least 30 minutes
- I will comfortably fit in size 34 pants
- I will no longer have a gut

FINANCIAL:
- I will earn an additional $3,500/month by the end of this year
- My debts will be paid off in the next 3 months: $20,000
- I will earn over $100,000 working part time so I can leave my job and concentrate on building my business with the goal of reaching $250,000 in my third year
- Within 5 years I want have saved enough to buy my 4 bedroom/2 bath dream house in New York for $850,000
- Within 5 years I want to help retire my parents by giving them $5,000 a month

SAMPLE AFFIRMATIONS:

Pick several, adapt if needed, and say them out loud when you wake up, during the day, and before you retire at night.

Affirmations for Prosperity:
[ ] "As of January 1st I have 20K in my bank account"
[ ] "I am now 35 and I own my own home!"
[ ] "My retirement account will have 2 million when I'm 65!"
[ ] "My income is constantly increasing"
[ ] "Abundance is mine"
[ ] "I will not quit!"
[ ] "I deserve all good in my life and that includes prosperity"
[ ] "I am a money magnet, and prosperity of all kinds is drawn to me"
[ ] "I know that life is abundant and I accept abundance in my life"
[ ] "My good comes from everywhere and everyone"
[ ] "Money flows to me from expected and unexpected sources"
[ ] "New opportunities to increase my income open up for me now"

Affirmations for Career:
[ ] "My unique and creative talents and abilities flow through me"
[ ] "There is a huge demand for my particular skills and abilities"
[ ] "I can pick and choose what I want to do"
[ ] "My work is enjoyable and fulfilling, and I am appreciated"
[ ] "I earn good money doing what I enjoy"
[ ] "Wonderful new opportunities are opening up for me to use my unique creative skills and abilities"
[ ] "I am successful at whatever I choose to do"

Affirmations for Joy:
[ ] "I go with the flow and my life is easy and filled with joy"
[ ] "I see the beauty in my surroundings and I radiate joy and love"
[ ] "I am grateful for all the wonderful things I already have in my life and those that are yet to come"
[ ] "As I learn to love myself I can feel the love and joy from my own heart flow through my body and radiate out to others"
[ ] "I increasingly relax and accept the good that I now know I deserve in my life"
[ ] "I regularly take time out to do the things I want and love to do, I follow my heart and feel a sense of freedom and release"
[ ] "I now choose thoughts that nourish and support me in a loving and positive way"

Affirmations for Health:
[ ] "I know that my healing is already in process"
[ ] "Every cell in my body vibrates with energy and health"
[ ] "I am healthy, healed and whole"
[ ] "I choose health"
[ ] "I naturally make choices that are good for me, I take loving care of my body and my body responds with health, an abundance of energy and a wonderful feeling of well-being"

Affirmations for Love:
[ ] "I am surrounded by love"
[ ] "I love and accept myself exactly as I am"
[ ] "I know that I deserve love and I accept it now"
[ ] "I am a loving, beautiful creative person and this is reflected in my relationships with others"
[ ] "Loving myself unconditionally brings healing and an abundance of love into my life"
[ ] "The love I give out returns to me multiplied"
[ ] "Love flows through my body, shines in my face and radiates out from me in all directions"

Affirmations for Relationships:
[ ] "I love and accept myself as I am knowing that by doing this I can love others more fully and they can love me"
[ ] "I make friends easily wherever I go"
[ ] "All my relationships are now loving and harmonious"
[ ] "I now attract the perfect partner into my life"
[ ] "I deserve love and happiness"
[ ] "I attract only loving and uplifting people into my life"
[ ] "My friends are mutually loving and supportive"
[ ] "The past has no power over me, I forgive all those that need my forgiveness and I forgive myself"
[ ] "I love and accept myself the way I am and I love and accept others in the same way"
[ ] "Everyone I come into contact with appreciates me for the wonderful person that I am"

Affirmations for Forgiveness:
[ ] "I forgive and I am forgiven"
[ ] "I easily forgive all those that need forgiving and I forgive myself"
[ ] "Forgiveness is a gift I now give to myself and those around me"

[ ] "The past has no power over me"
[ ] "Forgiving makes me feel light and free"
[ ] "The more resentment I release the more love I have to express"
[ ] "As I learn to love myself I find it easier to forgive"

Affirmations for Letting Go:
[ ] "I release all disease from my body and welcome health, love and happiness into my life"
[ ] "I release old hurt, anger and resentment easily"
[ ] "I choose to live my life the way that makes me happy and I am free"
[ ] "I release the need to be right all the time, to judge others and I am free"
[ ] "I choose to be in touch with my own needs and desires, I release the need to please others and know that I have a right to all my feelings and emotions"

ACTION ALERT #11:
TAKE ACTION ON YOUR AFFIRMATIONS!
CHOOSE & USE.

To some of you this may feel a little corny, to do this new-age mumbo jumbo ... but don't underestimate the power of the mind. It's time to rewrite the negative voices in your head and replace them with the power of positive energy.

But, of course, this is only the first step. Read on.

"The path to success is to take massive, determined action."
— **Anthony Robbins**

CHAPTER 34.
YOUR PERSONAL BUSINESS & LIFE
ACTION PLAN

ON-LINE WORKBOOK #6:
BUILD IT & IT WILL COME

Important Instructions:
• Use the on-line workbook to type up the draft of your business plan first. After all your revisions, the final draft should be in your own handwriting.
• Write the whole plan on a single side of one page.
• Keep the original plan with you and review it once a day.
• Make small copies containing your affirmations and goals/dreams and post them on your bathroom mirror and on your nightstand by your bed. When you wake up in the morning, and when you retire at night, read them. Visualize what your life is like now that you are living your dream. And then make it happen.

#1. Opening Statement For The Year:
Your theme "One Quote" followed by a one sentence of description
#2. Affirmations:
Transformative statements for yourself.
3-4 Sentences of your new image
Note: Affirmations should complement the rest of plan: strategies, Personal, self improvement, etc.
Less than 7-8 word per affirmation, preferably 4-6 words.
#3. Top 3-5 Reasons Why You Want To Be Successful: Must create strong, powerful feelings & emotions
Rules: intangibles, no numbers, no monetary amount. Its
Different than goals or dreams. Focus on WHY'S, Dig deep

Note: Hit the WHY'S (Top 3-5 reasons) then you'll hit goals & dreams.

#4. I. Dreams within This Year (Pick top 2 or 3 max)
- Be Very Very Very Specific
- Dream big and reasonable
- i.e.: Pay off debt: amount, quarterly dates
- Emergency funds: filled up
- Specific type, color, size of "Car" "house"
- Family: Vacation where? By when? About how much?
- Strategy is to hit your goals/dreams

#5. A. Personal: Make it VERY PERSONAL (Top 2-3 max)
This is about you "Self improvement/Self encouragement/Self motivation" Personal relationships
B. Physical: (Top 2-3 max)
Be specific with numbers, dates, time, amount, etc.
Put Schedules
C. Financial: (Top 2-3 max)
Income Goals, Savings, Pay off debts, net-worth. Set short, medium, long-term goals. Add by when using dates, amounts, etc

#6. Strategy: (Must support the goals & dreams, create a short, strong opening statement)
A. Intangible: (Pick top 2-3 max)
No numbers & amounts. It's how you'll handle the business/life.
B. Tangible: (Pick top 3-4 max)
"How to's?" What needs to be done to hit goals & dreams, etc.
C. Absolute Focus: (Pick top 1-2 max)
Zero in on these specific things & master it.
- Strategy is to hit your goals/dreams

II. Sacrifice & Penalty vs. Rewards (2-3 Things you'll do immediately)
- Be Very Very Very Specific
Sacrifice Example: Work Mon-Fri 6-10pm. TV in garage, Cut cable, Hang up favorite hobby, etc.
Reward Example: If hit Aug goals, than take 1 weekend trip. If not then in September work weekends.
Note: The sacrifices must be bigger than the dreams & rewards!

"Successful people have a social responsibility to make the world a better place and not just take from it."
— **Carrie Underwood**

CHAPTER 35.
THE SOCIAL RESPONSIBILITY MISSION:
US, YOU & THE PLANET.
GET INVOLVED. GET INFORMED. GET GOING.

Our Mission Explained: Children are the foundation for the stability, growth and ultimate success of society. Yet all too often they are not given the tools they need to succeed, especially regarding problems they inherit from previous generations.

"16 Things Kids Can Do" is a non-profit educational organization designed to provide an on-going network of books, programs, events and activities that educate and empower Kids, People and The Planet to be proactive throughout their lives on a host of fundamental issues ... subjects like health, nutrition, fitness, education, business, volunteering, the environment and life skills. And when kids and people are empowered, they can help change family and peer dynamics as well.

Imagine if you will, one kid that "gets it" on health & nutrition: When his parents offer to take him to a fast food place for dinner the second time that week, he or she declines, opting instead for something pre-made and healthier from the Supermarket.

Now, imagine that same kid turning down two or three opportunities a week to drink soda. And then telling his or her best friend not to drink so much also. And explaining why.

The Ripple Effect: Imagine the ripple effect this will have when these kids "get it" and begin using the same approach with friends and family ....

That's the power of "16 Things Kids Can Do" ... Books, Better Communication & Literacy Workshops, Programs, etc. that help Kids, People & The Planet "Get It" on a range of important issues.

But to make the impact we need for this type of sea-change, we need the support of you and your network. So, please take some time to join us in our efforts — whether it's in the form of volunteering, creating a club, writing a testimonial email, a link on your website, Facebook,

Twitter or You Tube pages or a donation of time or dollars — Every person counts and every bit helps.

I look forward hearing from you and seeing what we can do together to spread the word!

Lyle Benjamin,
Executive Director

"**16 Things Kids Can Do...** takes a unique approach to parenting
by engaging and empowering kids to learn and change behaviors
on their own without parental involvement. Guided by experts,
children learn to work through problems in constructive ways —
a process that firmly places them on the path toward
achieving the results they want in other areas of their lives!"
— **Mark Victor Hansen**

ACTION ALERT #12:
VISIT OUR ORG: WWW.16THINGSKIDSCANDO.ORG
GO TO "CONTACT US" & SHARE YOUR FEEDBACK!

16 THINGS PROGRAM GUIDE:

• **Reference Book Series:** Executive Director and Author, Lyle Benjamin, created a reference book series of over two dozen books each depicting 16 problems people encounter in specific areas of their lives, their normal unproductive responses, and "The Real Deal" — the steps they need to do and why — to solve the problems. Each problem is also addressed by two industry experts that give their testimony as to the why and how to address the issue. The books form a network of reference books that are used in "Better Communication & Literacy Workshops."

• **Better Communication & Literacy Workshops:** Each workshop is for up to ten kids and lasts eight to twelve weeks. Kids read out loud to the group the problems and then spend time discussing the collateral issues. Just like the reasons college students join fraternities and sororities, kids in the workshops benefit from peer support, social networking, and contacts for later on in life. When the workshops are for kids, no adults are allowed. BCL Workshops are available through schools, libraries and organizations.

• **National Kid's Month:** Presidential Proclamation Petition: "There is no question that as this generation of children grows into adults they will contend with the most difficult issues this country has ever faced over an extended period of time. While parents, schools and religious organizations do their best to educate their youth, there is no concerted effort to both engage the children in a unified systematic approach to the core issues while at the same time acknowledging, educating, and rewarding them for their efforts in exploring, learning, and working towards solutions to problems they effectively inherited.

Establishing the program in August coincides with children's, parents and school schedules and provides a pathway to growth, development, maturity and success that will have tremendous rewards during the school year and beyond.

We propose that each week in August focus on these key issues:
  Week 1: Health, Fitness, Nutrition & Wellness
  Week 2: Business, Finance & Life Skills
  Week 3: Literacy & Writing Skills
  Week 4: Volunteering, Mentoring & Public Service
The on-going goals of the program are to:
  1) Bring needed attention and education to these subjects
  2) Create mechanisms that encourage voluntary participation by kids
  3) Acknowledge said participation, and lastly
  4) Foster attitudes and environments that help perpetuate commitment to these issues

• **Internship, Work Experience & Career Track Programs:** The mission of our Internship Program is to provide opportunities for students and graduates to work on real world projects in order to develop their communication, business, office technology, marketing, management, leadership, research, problem solving and time management skills that will be of benefit to them both professionally and personally.

• **16 Things Social Responsibility Clubs:** Program works to establish and run clubs in colleges, high schools and communities that focus on diverse areas of interest that coincide with the Mission and programs of the organization. Clubs are all-inclusive and work to give members communication, administrative, business, management skills while provide valuable contents to members: Sub-Clubs include: 16 Things Book Club, Global Initiative Club, Social Responsibility Club, Library Club, Social Media Club, Health & Nutrition Club, Mentoring Club, Volunteer Club, Internship Club, etc. The focus of a Club may be limited to the school or community, or encompass the state, nation or globe depending on the objectives of each particular group. Clubs can work independently or network through the 16 Things Web Portal.

• **Community Based Educational & Work Programs:** We have the ability to create custom educational programs that can help your community address issues that are important to the well-being of youth and adults.

The following page is a program we developed for use with the Harlem, New York City based Youth Basketball Program "The League."

16ThingsKidsCanDo.Org

Lyle Benjamin, Exec. Director • 212 213-0257 • 917 683-2625
20 East Broadway, 4th Fl • New York NY 10002

Our Mission is to provide an on-going network of books, workshops, programs and activities that educate and empower Kids, People & The Planet to be proactive on a host of fundamental issues on subjects like education, finance, health, nutrition, business, the environment, volunteering and life skills. And when Kids & People are empowered they can create a ripple effect that can help change family, peer and world dynamics.

An Educational Non-Profit Organization Working for the Betterment of Kids, People & The Planet!

16 THINGS YOUTH & ADULT EDUCATION "PROGRAM GUIDE"

GENERAL INFORMATION:

Objective: To offer a series of classroom seminars, workshops and discussions designed to provide students with effective lifestyle education on important issues that influence their health, happiness and success in life.

Structure: Each topic is designed to be covered over consecutive classes.

Availability: Classes are available for different age groups on a daily basis at each site.

PROGRAM GUIDE:

Effective: **Elementary Students:**
- ❏ Art Program: Poster Contest "How Kid's Can Make The World Better Place!"
- ❏ Communication Program: Kids Learn Proper Communication Based On Numerous Contexts
- ❏ Literacy Program: Kids Read Out Loud About Topics And Then Discuss
- ❏ Financial & Business Literacy: How Money Works & Why You Need To Know

Engaging: **Middle School Students:**
- ❏ Communication Program: Kids Learn Proper Communication Based On Numerous Contexts
- ❏ Literacy Program: Kids Read Out Loud About Topics And Then Discuss
- ❏ High School Prep: Importance Of Being Well-Rounded
- ❏ Social Responsibility: Importance Of Living A Karmic Life (16 Things Clubs)
- ❏ Financial Literacy: How Money Works & Why You Need To Know
- ❏ Community Based Work Training Program: Communication, Business, Marketing, Time-Management

Empowering: **High School & College Students:**
- ❏ Communication Program: Kids Learn Proper Communication Based On Numerous Contexts
- ❏ Literacy Program: Kids Read Out Loud About Topics And Then Discuss
- ❏ Social Responsibility: Importance Of Living A Karmic Life (16 Things Clubs)
- ❏ College & Career Prep: Importance Of Being Well-Rounded
- ❏ The Keys To Success: Desire, Determination & Coach-Ability
- ❏ Financial Literacy: How Money Works & Why You Need To Know
- ❏ Community Based Work Training Program: Communication, Business, Marketing, Time-Management
- ❏ Career Track Opportunities: How To Pay For College While Attending College

Actionable: **Adults:**
- ❏ How To Properly Build A Million Dollar Retirement W/O Breaking Your Budget
- ❏ How The Best Selling Book "Rich Dad, Poor Dad" Can Change Your Life Without Even Reading It
- ❏ How To Give More To Your Church/Temple, Your Family & Your Retirement In 60 Days Or Less
- ❏ The Importance Of Volunteering & How It Can Change Your World

"Proactive giving is what you do when you've found your passion. It expresses your values, interests and concerns. It engages not just your dollars, but also your mind, time, skills and networks"
— **Laura Arrillaga-Andreessen**

CHAPTER 36.
FUND-RAISING FOR YOUR CHURCH, TEMPLE, SCHOOL, OR ORGANIZATION: WE CAN HELP — A LOT!

Want to raise funds for your group while helping them at the same time?

We have a whole host of programs:

• Books
• Seminars
• Workshops
• Partnerships
• Sponsorships
• Motivational Talks

In short, we've got you covered.

Call or email us and we'll be happy to help!

SECTION V:
SUPPLEMENTAL MATERIALS

"If a child, a spouse, a life partner, or a parent depends
on you and your income, you need life insurance."
— **Suze Orman**

CHAPTER 37.
THE UGLY, THE BAD & THE GOOD (& THEN SOME)

EXPLAINING "THE BIG THREE"
RISK MANAGEMENT & ASSET PROTECTION
LIFE INSURANCE PROGRAMS.

When getting the right coverage and benefits, insurance is a crucial part of your financial strategy. It's a good policy (pun intended) for you understand the differences between the major types of life insurance.

THE UGLY: Term Life Insurance: First issued in the 1880s, term life is the oldest form of life insurance, and the least expensive of the big three. It provides coverage for a limited period of time and if the client dies during the time the policy is enforce, the death benefit is paid to the designed beneficiary. After the term expires, the coverage is over. Think of term life as temporary insurance. Once expired, the individual can attempt to purchase new insurance based on his/her current age and health.

Pros: Very inexpensive when purchased by adults in their 20s and 30s. High death benefit to premium ratio. Any death benefit paid to the beneficiary while properly insured is Tax-Free.

Cons: Provides limited protection for a limited term and then expires. Very expensive to renew after expiration. And clients that want a better form of insurance will now find it too pricey to get the benefits they need from insurance later on in life. Finally, many clients have health issues during term coverage and become uninsurable after it expires.

Term insurance was made very popular by a company promoting **"Buy term and invest the difference."** Unfortunately, the vast majority of people that bought term insurance failed to invest the money they saved in premiums (as compared to Whole Life) and just squandered the savings away.

Group Life Insurance: Offered automatically by many companies to their employees through their benefits package is a form of Term life. The death benefit is usually low, around $50,000, and as long as you are employed by the company your coverage is intact. Switch jobs, get laid off or fired and your coverage is over.

Just remember a one time payment of $50,000 to your beneficiary is not going to provide more than funeral expenses and 3/4's of a year in college if you're lucky. In short, it's no replacement for the full monty.

THE BAD: Whole Life Insurance:

Pros: Unlike term insurance that expires after a predetermined time, Whole Life policies are guaranteed to remain in force for the insured's entire lifetime. Any death benefit paid to the beneficiary while properly insured is Tax-Free.

Cons: Fixed premiums must be paid for the entire life of the client, and are set based on the client's age and health at the time the policy was issued. Dividends are often offset by the high cost of insurance resulting in depressed cash accumulation. Often the fees charged by insurance companies to clients with Whole Life policies are difficult to determine. Assurances made by some insurance agents that clients can one day stop paying premiums may only provide temporary relief as the client may have to resume premium payments in future in order to prevent the policy from lapsing. Loans against the cash value have a relatively high rate of interest charged, and remain in effect until the borrowed money is paid back into the policy.

THE GOOD: Universal Life Insurance: UL is a type of permanent life insurance where the premium payments above the cost of insurance are credited to the cash value of the policy. The cash value is credited with interest based on the market or an index, and the policy is debited by the cost of insurance (COI) charge as well as any other policy charges and fees.

Pros: UL policies usually offer guaranteed level premiums at rates that are lower than Whole Life policies.

Universal life is similar in some ways to, and was developed from, whole life insurance, although the actual cost of insurance inside the UL policy is based on annually renewable term life insurance. The advantage of the universal life policy is its premium flexibility and adjustable death benefits. The death benefit can be increased (subject to insurability), or decreased at the policy owner's request.

The premiums are flexible, from a minimum amount specified in the policy, to the maximum amount allowed by the contract. The primary difference is that the universal life policy shifts some of the risk for maintaining the death benefit to the policy owner. In a whole life policy, as long as every premium payment is made, the death benefit is guaranteed to the maturity date in the policy, usually age 95, or to age 121.

Cons: A UL policy will lapse when the cash values are no longer sufficient to cover the cost of insurance and policy administrative expense.

THE BETTER: Variable Universal Life: VUL allows the cash value to be directed to a number of separate accounts that operate like mutual funds and can be invested in stock or bond investments with greater risk and potential growth. Additionally, there is the recent addition of index universal life contracts similar to equity-indexed annuities credit interest linked to the positive movement of an index, such as the S&P 500, Russell 2000, and the Dow Jones. To make UL policies more attractive, insurers have added secondary guarantees, where if certain minimum premium payments are made for a given period, the policy will remain in force for the guaranteed period even if the cash value drops to zero. These are commonly called "No Lapse Guarantee" riders, and the product is commonly called guaranteed universal life (GUL, not to be confused with group universal life insurance, which is also typically shortened to GUL).

THE BEST. Indexed Universal Life: (IUL) Interest that is tied to the market or several financial markets are call Indexed Universal Life policies. Unlike VUL, the cash value of an Index UL policy generally has principal protection, less the costs of insurance and policy administrative fees. Index UL participation in the index may have a cap, margin, or other participation modifier, as well as a minimum guaranteed interest rate.

Indexed life was first offered by Transamerica in 1997. Sales of these products were less than a half million that year, and have since surged to $539 million in 2008. There are 34 different insurance companies offering indexed life insurance today.

MISCELLANEOUS: The single largest asset class of all but one of the largest banks in the United States is permanent cash value life insurance, commonly referred to as **BOLI,** or **Bank Owned Life Insurance.** During the recent economic crisis, banks accelerated their purchasing of BOLI as it was the single most secure investment they could make. The majority of BOLI is current assumption Universal Life, usually sold as a single premium contract.

We all know how much banks love to make money. This should tell you something.

Read on.

"You Can Get Up To A Million Dollars Or More In
Life Insurance In Case You Die. But Can Only Get
About Seven Or Eight Bucks An Hour To Live"
— **Stanley Victor Paskavich**

CHAPTER 38.
HOW TO MAKE "THE GOOD, THE BAD & THE BETTER"
GREAT: THE 1035 EXCHANGE.

The great news is that if you have an existing Universal, Whole Life, or
Variable Life policy, it can be reviewed against a conparable IUL policy.
If it's in your best interest to stand pat, you don't make a change.

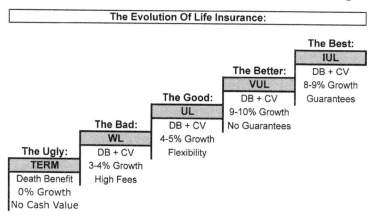

But if you can qualify for a better policy: One that has a higher cap or
a guaranteed floor, gets a better rate of return, has a higher death benefit, a lower monthly premium, a shorter time to pay in — you'll be
thrilled.

Either way, having the evaluation done is definitely worth your time.
Afterall, you are already doing this for your cell phone, right? Shouldn't
you be doing the same thing for yourself, your family and your future?

ON-LINE ACTION ALERT #13:
IT'S YOUR LIFE (INSURANCE) EVALUATON:
STAND PAT OR EXCHANGE & UPGRADE?

"I think that lawyers are terrible at admitting that they're wrong. And not just admitting it; also realizing it. Most lawyers are very successful, and they think that because they're making money ... they must be doing everything right."
— **Alan Dershowitz**

CHAPTER 39.
HOW TO BY-PASS LAWYERS THAT PUT PROFIT OVER CLIENT NEEDS

Have you ever had a problem and wished you had access to a lawyer that was on your side? Have you ever been out late at night and were stopped by the police. Did you wish you had someone you could call for help besides your friends and family?

Life happens, and it's expensive. And when problems or difficult situations come up, many times we end up hurting ourselves even more because (1) we don't have the expertise on how to solve them (2) they are expensive to fix.

Well, we have solution to these issues that won't break your bank: Unlimited legal advice from top rated law firms around the country, so you and your family have greater piece of mind to deal with life's "little" problems.

One consultation with a lawyer can cost upwards of $300. So many people don't get the help they need because it's too expensive.

After Hurricane Katrina, one of the homeowners was owed two checks totalling almost $100,000 by her insurance company. She desperately needed the money, and they were intentionally stalling. Most lawyers would have charged hundreds to get the situation resolved. Some would have charged a high percentage — as much as 30-40%!

But because she had her legal plan in place, her law firm made the calls and within a week she got both her checks. She received 100% of the money she was entitled to, and her legal fee was: $0.00

In your **Personal Plan, you get:**
• Coverage For You, Your Spouse/Partner And Dependent Children
• Unlimited Advice On Unlimited Personal/Business Topics
• Letters/Phone Calls On Your Behalf

- Legal Document Review
- Standard Will Preparation
- 24/7 Emergency Assistance
- Trial Defense (Not available in NY and Select States)
- Optional: Identity Theft Protection
- And the cost is less than $20 per month for a family plan.

Business Plans (for companies with 100 or fewer employees):
- Coverage includes:
- Unlimited Legal Consultation
- 30 Calls Or Letters Per Year
- 10 Collection Letters Per Month
- 30 Documents Reviewed Per Year
- Trial Defense Services (Not available in NY and Select States)
- Plans start at $39 depending on size of the company and coverage.

Take it from me, the reason why I quit the legal profession was because I felt it wasn't operating in the service of others. These programs give me some hope for the legal profession.

Remember a time when you were stopped by the police? Imagine giving them a card that reads, "NOTICE: If it is your intention to question, detain or arrest me, please allow me to call a lawyer immediately." And then has the toll-free number right there for you to call and talk to a lawyer.

That's legal protection that normally only the RICH can afford.

ON-LINE ACTION ALERT #14:
"CELEBRITY" LEGAL COVERAGE FOR THE REST OF US.

ON-LINE ACTION ALERT #15:
HOW MANY OF THESE "LITTLE" LEGAL ISSUES HAVE
YOU & YOUR FAMILY ENCOUNTERED?

Any one of these could have or might escalate into a "BIG" Legal issue. Acting on it after the horse has left the barn, is not the best way to protect your interests.

Mark 'em up and add 'em up! It's 'Round up time!
1. You don't want your credit ruined by being a victim of Identity Theft.
2. You need a will or you don't have an up-to-date will.
3. You do not have adequate retirement savings.
4. You don't understand your health insurance plan.
5. The IRS selects you for an audit.

6. Your parents die and leave you executor of their estate.
7. Family members challenge your parent's will.
8. You want to start a business but have enough capital or contacts.
9. You change jobs and need to rollover your 401(k) plan.
10. You receive a speeding ticket.
11. You are buying or selling your home.
12. Your driver's license is suspended.
13. Your landlord raises rent in violation of your verbal agreement.
14. Your teenager is accused of shoplifting.
15. You decide to change your name.
16. You don't understand the difference between a trust and a will.
17. Creditors threaten to take action against you for ex-spouse's debts.
18. A neighbor or school reports you for child abuse.
19. You adopt a child.
20. A friend or neighbor is injured on your property.
21. You need child support enforced.
22. A friend owes you money and files bankruptcy.
23. A stranger calls and demands money or will release damaging info.
24. Your car is damaged by a hit-and-run driver.
25. You accidentally back over a neighbor's garbage can.
26. A hairdresser damages your hair with harsh chemicals.
27. Your car is repossessed unjustly.
28. You are subpoenaed or served with legal papers.
29. You are called to jury duty.
30. Your long drive off the tee injures another player.
31. You need a lease agreement reviewed.
32. Your son is injured in a football game.
33. A neighbor trips over a rake in your yard.
34. A jeweler sells you defective merchandise.
35. A car dealership gains illegal access to your credit history.
36. You are hit by a bottle at a baseball game.
37. A tenant falls down stairs and sues you.
38. You need help with credit card liability resolution.
39. You are injured when you slip on a wet floor in a public building.
40. Your livestock trample a neighbor's garden.
41. Your neighbor's dog barks for hours every night.
42. Your teenager gets a speeding ticket.
43. Your landlord enters your apartment without permission.
44. Your child throws a baseball through a neighbor's car window.
45. You don't have a Living Will or Medical Power of Attorney.
46 - 101. The rest are on-line.
    Do your tally on-line, then read on!

"For a successful entrepreneur it can mean extreme wealth.
But with extreme wealth comes extreme responsibility ... to invest
in creating new businesses, create jobs, employ people, and to put
money aside to tackle issues where we can make a difference."
— **Richard Branson**

CHAPTER 40.
SOME STUFF YOU SHOULD BE AWARE OF .... AS AN
INDIVIDUAL ENTREPRENEUR OR AS A BUSINESS OWNER.

This chapter of the book is simply a brief overview of several programs that we should know about should the need arise. These subjects, and many others, are covered in the next A&GR Book: **"Act & Grow Rich For The Entreprenuerial Soul! The Business Owners Guide To Growing Rich & Staying Rich"** Afterall, no matter where we are on Kiyosaki's Cashflow Quadrant, we all should be acting like Entreprenuers if we want to acheive our goals and dreams. Right?

Annuities: How To Have A Guaranteed Income For Life. An annuity is a contract between you and an insurance company that is designed to meet retirement and other long-range goals. You make a lump-sum payment or series of payments to the insurance company, and in return you will receive periodic payments to you either immediately or at some future date.

Annuities typically offer tax-deferred growth of earnings at ordinary income rates, and may include a death benefit that will pay your beneficiary a specified minimum amount, such as your total purchase payments. There are generally three types of annuities — fixed, indexed, and variable.

Estate Planning: Planning Your Legacy. Estate planning can be defined as the accumulation, conservation, and distribution of an estate through a plan that will enhance and maintain the financial security of clients and their families.

In short, it's the process of giving what estate owners have, to the people or entitities they want, while determining when and how the transfer should occur in order to minimize administrative costs, transfer costs, and taxes.

Estate planning is not just a tool of the wealthy. Anyone that owns property, and wants to control, who, how and when the property is transferred at his or her death should engage in Estate Planning. The alternatives can be draining.

When Elvis Presley died suddenly in 1977, his estate was valued at $10 million. Because he didn't employ proper Estate Planning, after taxes and fees, his family inherited $2 million. His estate lost 80% of its value.

Executive Bonus Plans are when the employer purchases and pays for life insurance policies for a select group of employees via a pay raise to the employee(s) equal to the policy premium. In some cases employers add another bonus to cover the income tax on this additional pay.

Employees have full rights to the policy, its cash value, and can take tax-free income from the policy in the future.

Business Succession Planning is an absolute must otherwise everything you spent years to build up could come apart in the blink of an eye. When I had my printing and design business in Florida after I left law school, my father had a successful engineering practice in South Florida. Out of the blue, he approached me and offered to make me an equal partner in his company.

I was flattered, I told him, but perplexed. I was an English major and knew nothing about engineering. "That's just technical stuff. I know how your mind works. I can teach you that. What I can't find in my years of business is someone that has your communication skills and technical abilities that can handle clients properly."

I never took him up on his offer, and shortly afterwards I lost him in a plane crash. Because he was the driving force in his company, my family had no options other than shut it down. His business died with him. And that's a shame I still feel.

Business Owner Buy/Sell Agreements are absolutely necessary if you own a business or part of a business. Without it, a closely held or family business faces huge financial and tax problems on an owner's death, incapacitation, divorce, bankruptcy, sale or retirement.

A buy-sell agreement can prevent infighting by family members, co-owners and spouses, keep the business alive so its goodwill and customer base remain intact, and avoid cashflow problems that can follow.

Let's say, you and your partner Sue own a hotdog stand as 50/50 partners. Sue dies. Do you still have a business? Is Sue's husband or child your new partner? Do you have the right or the obligation to buy them out? If so, for how much and on what terms? Can you open up your own hotdog stand, or are you stuck with the old one? What if you die instead of Sue? These events are easy to handle with a buy-sell agreement, but very expensive without.

Whatever your questions, whatever your needs, we can help.

BIOGRAPHY:

Lyle Benjamin began his career as an Entrepreneur as an undergraduate English major when he founded The University of Florida's unofficial literary magazine. While attending law school, Benjamin was offered a job with the NY Attorney General's Office after completing his internship, but instead chose to leave school early to open a Printing and Design business.

Later Benjamin utilized his skills to create a best-selling relationship board game in partnership with a California game company. He then moved to New York City and successfully created, pitched and produced, "Relationships Today Magazine," the first national newsstand magazine exclusively devoted to helping people deal with the complexities inherent in all types of relationships: Intimate, family, friendship and work.

Benjamin's next endeavor was the creation of Locations, Etc. Inc., a Meeting and Special Events company that coordinated and managed over 50 different types of Corporate and Social events, and published a Special Events reference book sold in Barnes & Noble and other bookstores.

Social Responsibility issues again beckoned, and Benjamin changed the focus of his company to the Business Development of Start-ups that are designed to benefit Society on a larger level.

Principal among these companies is the not-for-profit educational organization, "16 Things Kids Can Do. Org" that works for the betterment of Kids, People and the Planet through an on-going network of books, programs, events and activities all designed to help people led happier, healthier, and more successful lives.

Benjamin is also working to establish career track programs that help people from all walks of life receive training and mentoring in the Financial Services industry with the ultimate goal of earning a six-figure income within one-three years, while building a career path that leads to financial independence, security, ownership and generational wealth.

REFERENCES:

1. http://www.mpaa.org/wp-content/uploads/2015/03/MPAA-Theatrical-Market-Statistics-2014.pdf
2. http://www.bls.gov/news.release/atus.t01.htm
3. http://www.reuters.com/article/2015/04/29/idUSnGNX4Ns8Pb+1d2+GNW20150429
4. http://www.tripadvisor.com/ShowTopic-g1-i12334-k5806062-How_much_time_do_you_spend_on_pre_vacation_planning-Holiday_Travel.html
5. http://www.dailymail.co.uk/femail/article-2703071/Brides-spend-36-days-planning-wedding-three-quarters-big-decisions-MET-groom.html
6. http://www.bls.gov/news.release/atus.t01.htm
7. www.politifact.com
8. www.wikipedia.org
9. www.answers.com
10. www.answers.com
11. www.fool.com
12. https://www.distractify.com/astounding-facts-about-how-we-actually-spend-our-time-1197818577.html 30 Surprising Facts About How We Actually Spend Our Time
13. http://www.investopedia.com/q
14. http://www.multpl.com/s-p-500-historical-prices/table/by-year
15. http://www.outsidethebeltway.com/history-of-american-income-tax-rates/
16. http://www.ncsl.org/research/health/state-policies-on-sex-education-in-schools.aspx
17. How Much Money do You Need to Retire? Tom Sightings http://money.usnews.com/money/blogs/on-retirement/2014/08/19/how-much-money-do-you-need-to-retire
18. Just How Many Baby Boomers are There? Kelvin Pollard and Paola Scommegna http://www.prb.org/Publications/Articles/2002/JustHowManyBabyBoomersAreThere.aspx
19. How Many Workers Support One Social Security Retiree? Veronique de Rugy http://mercatus.org/publication/how-many-workers-support-one-social-security-retiree
20. Private Sector Pension Coverage Fell By Half Over Two Decades, Economic Policy Institute, Monique Morrissey www.epi.org/blog/private-sector-pension-coverage-decline/